How to Record Books for Maximum Reading Gains

Marie Carbo, Ed.D.

Copyright Acknowledgement

Portions of *Bread and Jam For Frances,* © Copyright L. & R. Hoban, 1964, *Mouse Tales,* © Copyright A. Lobel, 1972, *I Hate School: How to Hang in and When to Drop Out,* © Copyright C. Wirths, M. Bowman-Kruhm, and P. Stren, 1987, and *Amelia Bedelia,* © Copyright P. Parrish & F. Siebel, 1963, were recorded and reprinted by arrangement with Harper & Row, Publishers, Inc.

A portion of *Teddy Bear, Teddy Bear* was recorded and reprinted by arrangement with Nellie Edge.

Portions of *The Emperor's New Clothes,* © Copyright V. Biro, 1985, and *Tales of South Asia: Legendary Creatures,* © Copyright B. Candappa, 1984, were recorded and reprinted by arrangement with The Wright Group.

A portion of the article "Gorbachev Says Change Will Sweep Bloc," © Copyright *The New York Times,* 1989, was recorded, and the entire article was reprinted, by arrangement with *The New York Times*.

A portion of the article "Hong Kong: Get it While it's Hot," from *Suitcase Talk,* © Copyright Traveling Times, Inc., 1989, was recorded and reprinted by arrangement with Traveling Times, Inc.

© Copyright Marie Carbo, 1989.

Published and Distributed by the National Reading Styles Institute, Inc., P.O. Box 39, Roslyn Heights, NY 11577.

All rights reserved. Unless as specified herein, no part of this publication or accompanying tape cassette may be reproduced, in whole or in part, stored in a retrieval system or transmitted in any form or by any means, electronic, mechanical, including photocopying, sound and/or image projection of any kind, without prior, express written permission from the publisher.

Library of Congress Cataloging in Publication Data

Carbo, Marie.
    How to record books for maximum reading gains / Marie Carbo.
      p.   cm.
    Includes bibliographical references.
    1. Individualized reading instruction. 2. Talking books.
  3. Reading--Remedial teaching. 4. Reading comprehension.
  I. Title.
  LB1050.38.C36   1989   372.4'3--dc20   89-29528

ISBN 0-929192-15-X

10 9 8 7 6 5 4 3 2

Printed in the United States of America

Table of Contents

Chapter 1   **Recorded Books = Remarkable Reading Gains** 1
Dramatic gains with average and at-risk students

Chapter 2   **How the Recorded Book Method Began** 7
A useful word-imprinting technique for children with severe memory disorders

Chapter 3   **How to Record Books For Maximum Reading Gains** 15
How to determine phrase length, pace and amount; how to record for a group, for one student, for older students and adults; step-by-step: how to record the books

Chapter 4   **How to Select the Books** 27
How to evaluate the quality of the writing; the student's language-comprehension level, reading level and interests; a Reading Interest Inventory™ you can use; why recorded books are important in whole-language programs

Chapter 5   **Sample Recordings For Groups and Individual Students** 37
Model recordings for students (grades 1 through adult)

Chapter 6   **Organizing the Teaching Materials and Grouping Students** 59
How to code the tapes, determine the amount to be recorded, how to monitor and adjust the recordings, store the materials, keep records

Chapter 7   **Using Recorded Books in the Subject Areas With Older Students** 69
(written by Sharon Briggs and Ginny Sorrell) Materials needed; tips for all recording, recording novels, recording textbooks, recommended books to record

Appendix A   **Designing Resources to Supplement the Book Recordings** 81

Appendix B   **Schedules and Record-Keeping Charts** 89

Appendix C   **Charts For Identifying Students' Favorite Books** 99

Appendix D   **Recommended Books For Tape Recording** 103

References 117

Chapter 1

Recorded Books = Remarkable Reading Gains

Why the Carbo Recorded Book Method™ Works

After using specially recorded books, many teachers find that their students advance in reading comprehension much faster than ever before — with many youngsters progressing at two to ten times their former rates! Probably the single most powerful and positive effect of the recorded book method is the fact that students can read back the recorded passage (which is always very *brief* and *above* their reading level), with a smoothness and fluency that they have never experienced. For many youngsters, their very first encounter with these recorded books begins to turn around their negative attitude about reading.

This transformation is almost immediate. The students hear themselves reading words they never read before, words they used to stumble over. They hear themselves reading easily and fluently. And, best of all, the entire process *feels* and *is* relatively effortless for the youngster. There are no furrowed brows and no feelings of "hard work," or embarrassment because of difficult words that must be decoded. After listening to a special recording of a book, while looking at the words in the book, the vast majority of students can read, with ease and enjoyment, books that are well above their reading level.

The recorded book method is easy for educators to learn, and effective. High-interest books are divided into short segments. Then each segment is recorded on a separate tape side, in short phrases, at a fairly slow rate. The student listens repeatedly, and soon thereafter, reads that passage aloud to the teacher. Chapter 3 describes the method in detail.

Reading Strides Made in the Regular Classroom

The recorded book method has been so successful that many classroom teachers report their biggest problem to be keeping up with the pace of the children. Typical of the comments made, is this one by Janet Davis, a classroom teacher:

> *They come in each morning clamoring for their turn at the tape recorder!...The most exciting part to me was the immediately noticeable improvement in their reading ability. The boys also enjoy sharing a page or two...after every listening they're showing off their skill! They're so proud!*

Courtesy, Howard County Schools, Maryland

Dramatic Gains in Achievement by At-Risk Students

Hundreds of teachers have reported remarkable reading gains using reading styles techniques that emphasize the recorded book method. The most successful reading styles programs identify students' strengths, such as perceptual abilities and global or analytic thinking style, and then use reading methods, materials and strategies that "match" the child's strengths (Carbo, 1987). The recorded book method matches the reading styles of many at-risk youngsters. One of the most dramatic successes was reported by Joan Williamson, a teacher of American Indian tenth graders. When Williamson introduced reading styles and recorded books into her program, her students shot up two years in reading comprehension in just two months, compared to a gain of two months in reading comprehension during the previous two months. After the first ten months of the reading styles program, some students had gained four and five years in reading comprehension!

Some poor readers gain in leaps...

When Lois LaShell was a resource teacher, her handicapped students made such rapid gains in reading that she had difficulty recording enough books for them: LaShell wrote:

> *As it is, I can't keep up with the recordings. The kids go faster than I – they are becoming more and more excited about "how many" books they can read, and some are moving way ahead in jumps.*

At the end of that school year, LaShell reported that 37 of her 40 handicapped students had achieved mainstreaming scores in reading, compared with only 2 out of 40 the previous year (LaShell, 1983).

Children who hated reading begin to argue over books...

Identical experiences were described by both LaShell and Hodges after working with two different groups of at-risk youngsters (Carbo, 1983). Helenè Hodges was the director of a school for twice-retained, inner-city seventh graders reading about 5 years below grade level, while LaShell taught handicapped, elementary-aged students. Both educators found that their students changed dramatically – from a fear to a love of reading – after each implemented a total reading styles program which emphasized the recorded book method. A substitute teacher for LaShell wrote:

> ...the thing that amazed me over and over again was how the kids loved to read. They lined up to read to the parent volunteers or high school students and would argue over who got to read next.

Hodges made a similar observation:

> ...the children actually began arguing over the books because there were some that they all liked so much.

Severely Handicapped Children Learn to Read

The recorded book method described in Chapter 3 has made readers of youngsters who many thought would never learn to read. Carol Sullivan, a gifted speech therapist, used the recorded book method with an autistic student, and with a retarded youngster having a 71 I.Q. Both youngsters attained a third-grade reading level. In a conversation I had with Sullivan in 1989, she made these profound observations about why the recorded book method works so well with severely handicapped children, especially those with auditory disorders.

The importance of pacing...

> The special book recordings help the children to pace their auditory processing. Many of the kids can't retrieve language quickly so they use fillers, like, "uh." They're buying time for retrieval and to formulate their thoughts. The recording helps them to co-pace with the tape. It paces for them. It gives them the pacing as a metronome does. The reader who tapes sets the pace for that particular child, and gives a good, clear speech model.

Why some students aren't good at phonics...

> Some kids are not good at phonics probably because they have problems in auditory sequencing. Their short-term memory isn't good. Many have fluid in the middle ear. It sounds as if they're listening under water. The ear infections come and go. The fluids come and go. They've learned not to depend on their auditory sense. Unconsciously, they use their visual sense.

What the tape recordings do...

For kids with impaired speech or phonological disorders, the tape recordings eliminate stumbling. They eliminate the need to see and formulate words correctly. They eliminate much of the tension. The student isn't burdened with decoding the word. Many kids with auditory problems have delayed speech production. The tapes give these kids the little words, and the word endings they have difficulty hearing.

Don't worry, you'll be safe...

The tape also says to them: Listen to this. Don't worry. You'll be safe. I have confidence you can do it. Maybe not now, but you will.

Even high-risk students with extreme problems have learned to read...

Angela Haller, a graduate student of Lois LaShell's used the recorded book method and successfully taught a child to read who had only one side of his brain intact. The youngster's physicians thought that he would never learn to read. Haller wrote:

For my project, I am using the recorded book method with Renee Fuller's Ball-Stick-Bird series with a nine-year-old boy who is missing about half of his left hemisphere, due to surgery for a brain tumor. I alternate the BSB books with folk tales. I have been excited to see him change. He truly enjoys reading now. There can be no doubt that the recorded book method is responsible for his success.

Recorded Books = Increased Student Motivation and Self-Esteem

Time and time again, teachers have found that students who formerly hated to read aloud, *want* to read aloud, and do it with confidence, after using the recorded books. In fact, many poor readers ask to read aloud to anyone who will listen to them.

I recall visiting a first-grade classroom in the Shoreline School District in Washington. The program was developed by Kathy Hitchner and June Dallaire, and was based on reading styles and the meaning-driven reading model of David Adams and Jim Worthington. I sat in the back of the room and watched the children working. One little girl came near me to get a book and recording. She asked me if I would like to hear her read. I said that I would love to. She sat down next to me and read the story to me. Her reading was just a little slow, but she was able to read all the words confidently, and was obviously enjoying herself.

Even slow readers are open, secure and confident...

Midway into the book, her classmates began to assemble in the front of the room for a lesson with their teacher. The little girl continued to read the story to me. I told the child that I had enjoyed her reading very much and that perhaps she should join her class. She looked up, nodded and smiled, put the book away, and joined her classmates. Later, her teacher told me that that child was the lowest reader in the class. I marveled at the confidence that the youngster had, and the sense of security which had enabled her to read aloud in such a relaxed manner to a total stranger. This is how all children should feel about reading – relaxed, confident, and enthusiastic. And this is how they *can* feel if teachers match their reading styles, which often means using the recorded book method.

Courtesy, Robert W. Carbonaro School, District 24, Valley Stream, NY.

Courtesy, Robert W. Carbonaro School, District 24, Valley Stream, NY.

Chapter 2

How the Recorded Book Method Began

I developed the recorded book method in 1974 for a group of learning disabled students in grades one through six. The youngsters had been struggling with phonics for years. They had memory problems, auditory perception deficits, and had difficulty paying attention (Carbo, 1978a). They could not discriminate easily among sounds, or blend them to form words. Their attention and memory deficits made it difficult for them to recall whole words. As a result, their sight vocabulary was minimal and their reading was labored. I wanted to give the children sufficient practice in reading well-written books of their own choice, and at the same time develop an approach that would prove to them that they were *capable* of learning to read.

The First Breakthrough

The first breakthrough occurred with a child named Georgette. Georgette was repeating second grade and could not read one single word, not even her own name. I had tape recorded the first four words of a pre-primer story with her, and provided several strategies on the recording to help her remember the words (Carbo, 1978b). (The specific strategies are described later in this chapter.) Georgette was given the recording and the word cards one morning, and was advised to return to her classroom and listen to the recording while looking at the word cards, as many times as she liked. When she returned to me that afternoon she was able to read all four words *and spell them* correctly on the chalkboard! The next day, I recorded the first pre-primer story which contained those four words, using a fairly slow pace and good expression. Georgette followed along in the pre-primer while she listened to the 1½-minute recording. She repeated this process four times and then read the story back to me with good fluency. Because Georgette's memory deficiencies were severe, as a third step, I placed phrases from the story on a card reader and in matching games for additional practice. (See Appendix A for specific procedures.)

Experimenting With Two Different Recording Approaches

During the following several months, Georgette gained steadily in her reading skills. Based on her successes, I decided to experiment with two different recording approaches with eight of the children. For the first three months I used lengthy book recordings that I had made for the students. Each tape side contained about 15 to 20 minutes of text. For the subsequent three months I made and used brief recordings – about one to four minutes of text per tape side. The longer recordings resulted in a three-month gain in word recognition, for those students, during a three-month period. My results were similar to those reported by Chomsky (1976) with the commercial recordings she used with poor readers in third grade. I found, as had Chomsky in her experiment, that my students needed to follow along with a lengthy recording many times (about 5 to 20 repetitions over a period of a few weeks), before they could read portions of the text with any fluency.

Why the Brief Recordings Were Superior With At-Risk Students

Listening repeatedly to brief recordings, rather than to longer ones, proved to be far more effective because the children could immediately read back a short passage after listening to a cassette just two or three times. The process of reading silently while following along, several times, with a two- to three-minute recording, and then reading aloud and discussing that portion of the story required a total of only 15 to 20 minutes. The students became excited about the program and literally begged for more book tapes.

After two months of using the brief recordings, their reading improvement was phenomenal! The students' average gain in word recognition was 8 months. The highest gain was 15 months and the lowest was 4 months. The slow-paced, brief recordings of high-interest books, which were above the students' reading levels, produced much higher reading gains than those reported by Chomsky (1976), whose poor readers were allowed to listen repeatedly to lengthy passages or, those reported by Torgesen, Dahlem and Greenstein (1987), whose learning disabled subjects listened only once to brief recordings of a text.

Georgette: The Inspiration For the Recorded Book Method

The child who, in effect, inspired the recorded book method was Georgette. I developed both the word imprinting procedure and the recorded book method while working with this child. For those who are working directly with youngsters like Georgette, or who are responsible for directing their instructional programs, I advise that you try the word imprinting method described later in this chapter. This method has been particularly effective with students who are reading on a very low level, and who have memory deficits. Most youngsters can learn to read well with the recorded book method described in Chapter 3, and will not need the imprinting technique, which is rather time consuming. Some students may need supplementary materials, such as those described in Appendix A. Youngsters like Georgette will need it all — the word imprinting method, book tapes, and supplementary materials.

Searching For a Method to Help Georgette

Georgette's auditory perception made it difficult for her to discriminate among similar sounds, so I ruled out a phonics-type method for her. Georgette was somewhat stronger visually than she was auditorially, but she still needed a great many repetitions before words became sight words. Since her main problem was one of memory, I decided to start with a basal pre-primer that contained a highly controlled, repetitive vocabulary. This was a difficult decision to make because children with poor memory need high-interest reading material, and the basal pre-primer was far from interesting. I decided, however, that for only this initial stage, Georgette needed the consistent repetition, and slow building of vocabulary that the pre-primer offered. As soon as possible, Georgette was moved into high-interest storybooks (halfway through the primer).

While developing Georgette's reading program, I reasoned that if I could record the words that she would see in her first story, and if I could provide sufficient multisensory repetition of those words, Georgette might be able to retain the words.

Figure 2-A. In this photo, Georgette was well on her way to becoming a competent reader. Here she shares her storybook with her favorite doll, "George," to whom she loved to read. Notice that Georgette is "playing" at being the teacher by tracing her finger under the words for George, just as she had been taught.(Courtesy, Robert W. Carbonaro School, Valley Stream, NY.)

Figure 2-B. Informal reading areas help children to relax and become more open and receptive to learning. (Courtesy of the Butcher Children's School, Emporia, KS).

Planning the Method For Georgette

Three weeks from the day that I met Georgette she began to read. I started by writing the four words in Georgette's pre-primer story on separate, large cards. I pressed down heavily with a crayon so that Georgette would be able to feel the contour of the letters when she traced over them. The word cards were then numbered sequentially to enable Georgette to use them later, independently. I devised six procedures for imprinting the words in Georgette's memory.

Six procedures for imprinting the words
1. Seeing and saying the word by imitating the teacher
2. Establishing word meaning
3. Increasing awareness of word configuration
4. Experiencing the word tactually
5. Associating symbol with sound
6. "Picturing" the word

Georgette's First Recording

Georgette and I made a joint tape recording that she could listen to in her classroom and at home. To record all four words took about ten minutes. Georgette returned to her classroom with her word cards, tape player and headset. I taught her how to use the tape player and headset, and then asked her to follow the directions on the tape recording, and to listen to the recording as many times as she needed in order to learn the four words. Since the tape player operated on batteries, Georgette could work anywhere in her classroom. A separate desk in an isolated section of the classroom was provided.

Immediate Success

When Georgette returned to the resource room at 1:00 pm, she was smiling broadly and was able to read every one of the four words to me rapidly and effortlessly. Then she asked, "Do you want to see me write them on the board?" She proceeded to write each of the four words perfectly on the chalkboard. Here, now, is a portion of the first tape recording, which enabled Georgette to learn the four words, exactly as I recorded it with Georgette. (The next section is adapted from, "A Word Imprinting Technique For Children With Severe Memory Disorders," by Marie Carbo, *Teaching Exceptional Children*, Fall 1978.)

The Word Imprinting Technique That Led to the Recorded Book Method

Seeing and saying the word by imitating the teacher

Teacher: Georgette, can you find the card with the number "one" on it?
Georgette: Here it is.
Teacher: Good. That is the word *ride* (teacher moves her finger from left to right below the word *ride*).
Georgette: *Ride* (repeating the teacher's hand gesture).
Teacher: Fine.

Establishing word meaning
Teacher: Georgette, have you ever gone for a ride?
Georgette: Well...I ride in my car.
Teacher: Good.
Georgette: And I ride my bike.
Teacher: Fine.

Increasing awareness of word configuration
Teacher: Now let's look at the word *ride*. Notice that the first two letters are even. (Teacher moves her finger across the top of the *r* and the *i* .)
Georgette: Then it goes up and then down again. (Georgette moves her finger up to the top of the *d* and down to the *e* .)
Teacher: Very good, Georgette. Let's trace around the word *ride* again. First we move across the two short letters, then up to the tall letter, and down to the last short letter. (Teacher moves her finger around the perimeter of the top of the word.) Can you do that?
Georgette: (Nodding her head and imitating the teacher's previous gestures.) Here's the two little letters. Then I go up this one and down this one.
Teacher: Fine. Notice that the bottom of the word is even. (Teacher moves her finger from left to right under the base of the word while Georgette imitates her gesture.) Good.

Experiencing the word tactually and associating symbol with sound
Teacher: Now I'm going to show you how to trace the letters in the word *ride*. Trace over the word this way. (Teacher places the index finger of her writing hand on each letter, and then moves her finger in the correct direction.) Would you like to try?
Georgette: (Traces with her finger over each letter.)
Teacher: Good, Georgette. *Rrrid* .(Teacher traces over each letter with her index finger, as she vocalizes its corresponding sound.) *Rrrid*. That's the silent *e*.
Georgette: Rrrid (tracing each letter and vocalizing each corresponding sound). That's the little silent one. (Georgette points to the *e* .)
Teacher: Fine. That's right. That is the little silent *e*. That's excellent.

Picturing the word
Teacher: Now Georgette, look at the word *ride* very carefully.
Georgette: I'm looking at it.
Teacher: Good. Try to picture it in your mind. I'm going to ask you to remember it with your eyes closed. No, not yet. You may keep your eyes open now. Look at the word *ride*. Try to remember the whole word.
Georgette: I think I know it.

Teacher: Fine. Now, close your eyes. Can you picture the word *ride* ? Do you see it in your mind? (Georgette nods her head.) Show me what you see. Write the word *ride* in the air.
Georgette: (With her eyes closed, Georgette writes the *r* in the air and vocalizes the *r* sound). *R r r.*
Teacher: And the next short letter...
Georgette: (Writing the *i* and *d* in the air and vocalizing their corresponding sounds), *Id.* And the little silent *e.*
Teacher: Georgette, that's wonderful. Open your eyes. What word did you just write?
Georgette: (Happily) *ride* !
Teacher: You did very well. I'm proud of you.

Combining the Word Imprinting Method and the Recorded Book Method

Georgette was very happy and wanted to learn more words. That night, I let her take the tape recording and word cards home, along with ways to practice the words in her notebook and in some simple games. The next day, I gave Georgette a recording of the first pre-primer story which had the four words she had learned the day before. I had recorded the story slowly on one tape side, using a pace and phrasing that Georgette would be able to follow. The entire recording took about 1½ minutes. Georgette listened to the recording four times and followed along in the book. Then she read the story aloud to me with no difficulty whatsoever.

After the first two weeks, I would place the new words on one tape side, and the new story on the reverse side of the tape cassette. Georgette was sometimes able to complete both tape sides in one day. I also supplemented the tapes with audio cards, games and worksheets, which are described in Appendix A. During a four-week period, Georgette learned 31 words. It became apparent to me that the tape recording procedure was successful because it helped Georgette to focus on the task, provided sufficient repetition, interested her, and increased sensory input.

Why Georgette Remembered the Words

Georgette had severe memory difficulties, and the word imprinting and recorded book methods had helped her to read with relative ease, compared to her previous performance. But why? I believe it is because the methods that I used took into account four important factors which affect memory:

Four Factors That Affect Memory (Lerner, 1971)
1. Intensity of attention
2. Meaningfulness of material
3. Degree of interest
4. Amount of drill or overlearning

To Lerner's list, I would add:

5. Amount of positive reinforcement
6. Environmental factors that may help or hinder learning (e.g., sound, light, temperature and design)

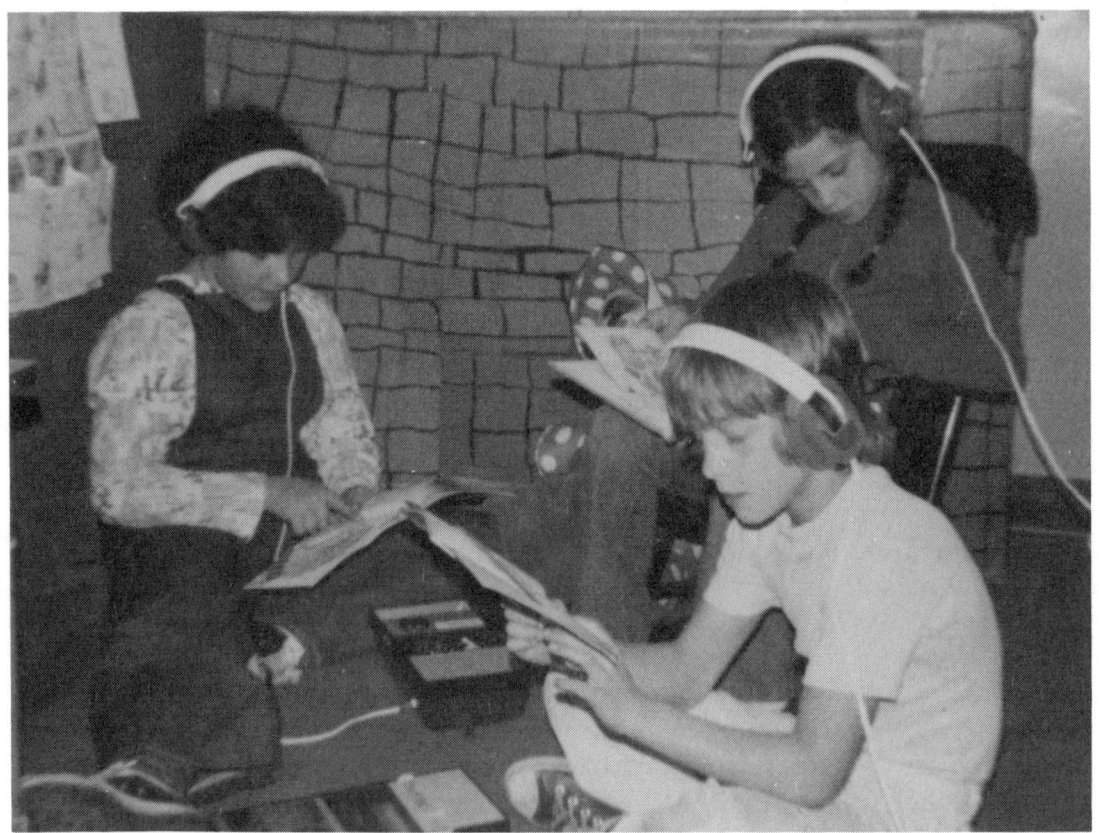

Courtesy, Robert W. Carbonaro School, District 24, Valley Stream, NY.

Chapter 3

How to Record Books For Maximum Reading Gains

Description of the Method
The recorded book method is simple, inexpensive and can be incorporated into any reading program. This method of recording differs from others in that *very* small amounts of text are recorded on one tape side, at a slower-than-usual pace, with good expression. This procedure has enabled even the poorest readers to master, and read back fluently, passages that are well above their reading level. Any reading material that is of interest to the student can be recorded. The length of the recorded text, and the reading rate of the person recording, depend on four factors described later. The student listens repeatedly to the brief passage, and then reads that passage, or a portion of it, aloud to the teacher, preferably within a few minutes.

What the Recordings Do For the Student
The slow recordings synchronize for the reader the spoken words with the printed text, while the repetition of small amounts of text greatly facilitates word retention. The short, natural phrases translate the printed page into meaningful segments; and the pauses help to increase word recognition and comprehension. In effect, the person who records the passage sets the pace for the reader, in much the same way as a metronome does for a musician. The tape recording provides a good, clear speech model. As discussed in Chapter 1, for children with low language proficiencies, and/or impaired speech or phonological disorders, this model can be crucial. Many children have improved in both their speech patterns and in their writing ability after working with the book tapes for a few months. Well-written texts that are of great interest to students have produced the largest gains.

The recorded book method has been particularly effective with youngsters who have difficulty learning with phonics, and with older students and adults who are "turned off" to reading. Most students experience quick success, which builds their self confidence, and sharply increases their motivation to learn to read. The recordings enable older students and adults to read material on their language-comprehension level, and helps them to integrate the rhythm, rate and natural flow of language so necessary for good comprehension.

Four Variables Controlled by the Person Recording

To assure that a youngster will be able to read back a recorded passage with fluency and ease, the recorder needs to control these four variables:

1. The amount recorded
And the recorder's
2. Pace
3. Phrasing
4. Expression

The simple key is this:

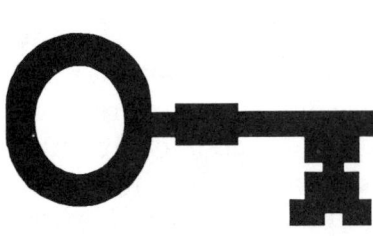

IF THE GAP BETWEEN THE STUDENT'S READING LEVEL AND THE LEVEL OF THE BOOK IS SMALL, RECORD ABOUT FIVE TO FIFTEEN MINUTES OF A STORY ON ONE TAPE SIDE AT A FAIRLY NORMAL PACE, WITH NATURAL EXPRESSION AND PHRASING. IF THE GAP IS LARGE, USE A SLOWER PACE, FEWER WORDS TO A PHRASE, EXAGGERATE YOUR EXPRESSION, AND RECORD MUCH LESS – ABOUT TWO MINUTES.

How to Select the Books

To be most effective, the books selected for the recorded book method should be *above* the student's reading level, and at or above the youngster's language-comprehension level. Chapter 4 discusses in greater depth how to select books to record for a student.

Importance of Recording Small Amounts

Since the books that are recorded should be *above* the student's reading level, most students will need to listen to a tape side more than once to be able to read back the material fluently. That is why only about two to five minutes of text should be recorded on each tape side. Text is recorded in small, sequential portions, so that pages 1-8 might be on the first tape side, pages 9-14 on the second, pages 15-21 on the third, and so on. A short picture book might take four tape sides to complete, while a longer book could take twenty tape sides.

Determining Phrase Length, Pace, and Amount

Many poor readers cannot keep up with the pace of commercially-recorded books because too much has been recorded on one tape side at too fast a pace. Often the recordings have too few or unclear page cues and distracting sound effects. Both the reading rate and phrase length of the person recording, depend upon the reading ability of the potential listener. For example, if an upper grader with poor reading skills chooses a difficult book, the selection should be recorded using short phrases (two to four words per phrase), at a slower-than-usual rate (65 to 80 words per minute), and in small amounts (as little as one paragraph). The length of the recorded passage (from one paragraph to about five pages) will depend upon the amount of material that the potential listener can digest in one sitting, and then read back with relative ease, as observed on several trials.

As the youngster's reading improves, the recording pace should be *gradually* quickened, the phrases lengthened, and the amount increased. If a student chooses a recorded book below his/her reading level (which is rare for poor readers), then the material should be recorded at a normal rate, in longer phrases, and in larger amounts.

Summary
When recording for a student or a group, consider the:
- Degree of interest in the book,
- Maximum phrase length that can be assimilated,
- Maximum reading rate that can be followed easily,
- Amount of reading material that can be digested in one sitting.

How the Student Works With the Tapes

The student should listen about two or three times to one tape side that usually contains a one- to five-minute recorded passage. Then, within minutes, the youngster reads that passage aloud to someone. The "someone" could be a teacher, parent, peer, or a volunteer. If the person recording has used the correct pace, phrasing and expression, and has recorded the correct amount, the student should be able to read the recorded passage aloud after listening to it a few times. After reading the passage aloud and discussing it, some students may be able to move on to the next tape side, which would contain the next portion of the story. It is not necessary for the student to read back an entire passage, but a sufficient amount should be read aloud to ensure that the youngster has mastered the text.

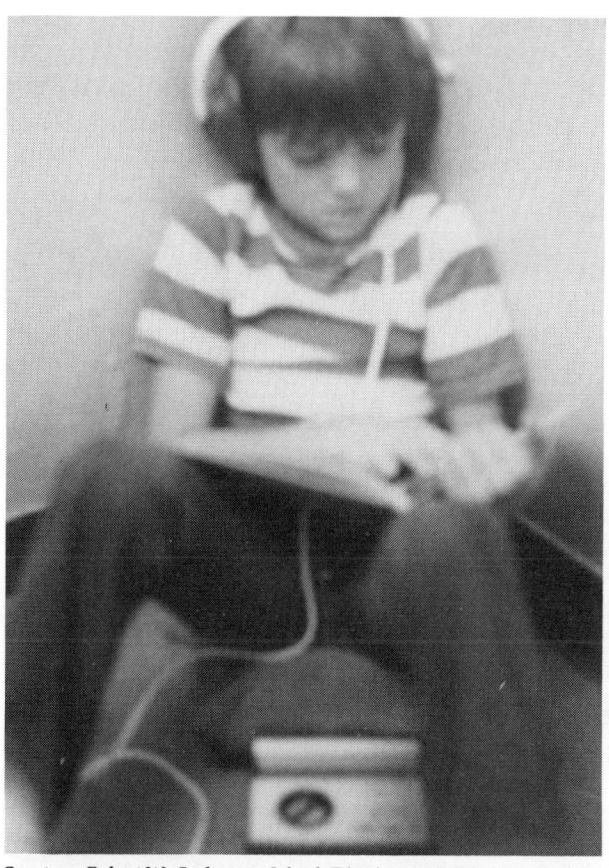

Courtesy, Robert W. Carbonaro School, District 24, Valley Stream, NY.

When a Student Cannot Read Back a Passage With Ease

How can you tell whether you have synchronized the printed and spoken words for a child and recorded the right amount? After listening to a recording about two to three times, the student should be able to read that section back fluently with no more than about two or three errors. Since every rule does have its exceptions, there may be some strongly motivated students who will make excellent progress after four repetitions of a tape recording. Generally, however, if a youngster needs more than three repetitions of a book tape, the book may be too difficult or it may not have been recorded correctly for that student. Either an easier book should be selected for the student, the amount of text that the child needs to master should be reduced, and/or the passage should be recorded at a slower pace.

As a first step toward correcting a tape recording, the student can be asked how the recording can be improved. If the student is *highly motivated* to read the book, make a special recording of a small portion using short phrases and a slow pace. If the student can read back the difficult book after about three to four repetitions, then the special recordings should continue to be made.

Rather than re-record a passage when a youngster cannot read it back smoothly, a second possibility is to alter the directions given to the youngster. Say: "Listen to the entire tape once. Then listen to just the _____ (first paragraph, first page, whatever amount seems reasonable for the student), another two or three times." Reducing the amount of text that the youngster should master, allows many students to read back successfully what may have been, otherwise, difficult or impossible.

If the student continues to read back the passage in a very halting manner, or cannot read some of the words, the level of the book may be too difficult. An easier book should be recorded for the youngster.

Figure 3-A. If the student cannot read back the passage, ask the youngster to listen to the entire recording once, and then re-listen a few more times to just the beginning portion of the recording. It is that small portion that the student masters and reads back.

How to Use the Same Recording With Students of Differing Abilities

If the recording is too easy – If the youngster needs no repetitions of a recorded passage, or can read the book fluently without listening to a recording, the student should move on to a more difficult book – *unless* the youngster wants to listen to the recording for enjoyment or reinforcement. In that case, allow it, but at the same time encourage the student to move on to higher level books as soon as possible.

If the recording is too difficult – Even if a recording of a book has the correct pace and expression, some youngsters may not be able to read the recorded passage after listening to it as many as four times, while following along in the book. In such cases, usually too much has been recorded on one tape side for these students. As described previously, they should be directed to listen to the entire recording once while following along in the book, and then to re-listen two or three times to just a small section of the beginning of the passage another two or three times - such as the first paragraph or page. Then the youngster should be asked to read back just that beginning portion which he/she listened to repeatedly. If the reading is still labored, then probably an easier book should be recorded.

When Should Students "Sound Out" Words They Don't Know?

One of the purposes of the recorded book method is to *eliminate* the need for students to decode words and to increase reading comprehension and fluency. Those youngsters who cannot sound out a word easily should be told the unknown word. If a child has the auditory and analytic skills to decode a word, and wants to, then encourage it. If more than three words are missed by a student, when reading back, one more repetition of the tape should be tried (four should be a maximum for most students). Separate phonics lessons may be provided for those youngsters capable of learning with that method.

Are Students Merely Memorizing Words?

The recorded book method is so simple and effective that a few educators have questioned whether the student is "just memorizing the words." But that is what we all do to widen our vocabulary. Most important, generally, there is excellent word retention and there *is* transference to other reading materials and to reading tests. Although students may not be able to read a difficult book without the aid of a tape recording, as the youngsters continue to work with the book tapes, they will begin to read independently books of increasing difficulty. Moreover, they demonstrate large gains in reading comprehension and word recognition on standardized reading tests.

Providing Extra Practice of the Words in the Recorded Passage

Some youngsters may need more practice of the words in the recorded passage before advancing to the next tape. Like Georgette, whose memory deficiencies were described in Chapter 2, they may need to practice words or phrases using devices such as flash cards, card readers, games or worksheets. Those students might practice the words and phrases for a day or two before proceeding to the next tape side. Appendix A contains specific strategies for providing word practice.

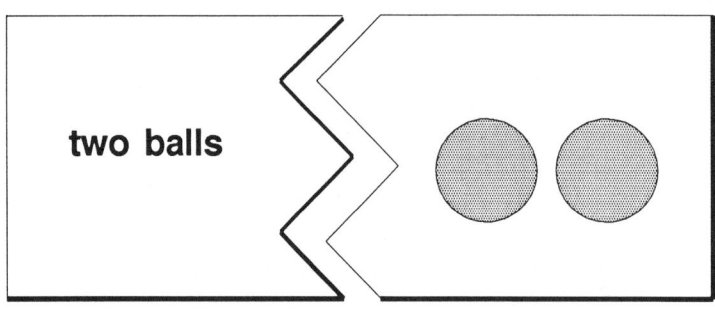

Recording More Than One Passage Per Tape Side

Some teachers have been successful in recording a few passages per tape side and training children to use a counter that is on the tape recorder. It is important to remember, however, that this method requires a great deal of rewinding and re-listening. Often, many youngsters lose their place if a counter is used, and this may cause confusion. Most teachers have found it efficient to place only one small portion of text on each tape side.

How to Begin and End a Recording

Start a recording by stating the name of the book, and telling the student something about the book. Sometimes the back cover of the book may have a description that can be used. This introduction should be *very* brief since the students will hear it more than once as they re-listen to the tape.

After the passage is recorded, end the tape by telling the listener something about the next passage of the story. For example, a recording might end this way: "We'll find out what happens to Joe on his first day of school on the next tape side." Pause, and then say, "Please rewind the tape for the next listener. That ends this recording."

Importance of the Attitude of the Teacher

When the student reads back a passage, the attitude of the teacher should be positive, receptive and encouraging. The teacher's body language, facial expressions and tone of voice are extremely important. The teacher should sit in a relaxed manner next to the student, and use an accepting, fairly soft voice. While reading back a passage, if the youngster cannot read a word immediately, the teacher should wait a few moments, and give the youngster a little time. Unknown words should be provided by the teacher in a quiet, unobtrusive manner. Note: If a student has listened to a recording twice, and makes more than two or three errors, or reads in a slow, halting manner, another repetition or two of the tape recording may be needed.

Figure 3-B. A student reads a story to the author with well-deserved pride in her accomplishment. (Courtesy, Carbonaro School, Valley Stream, NY).

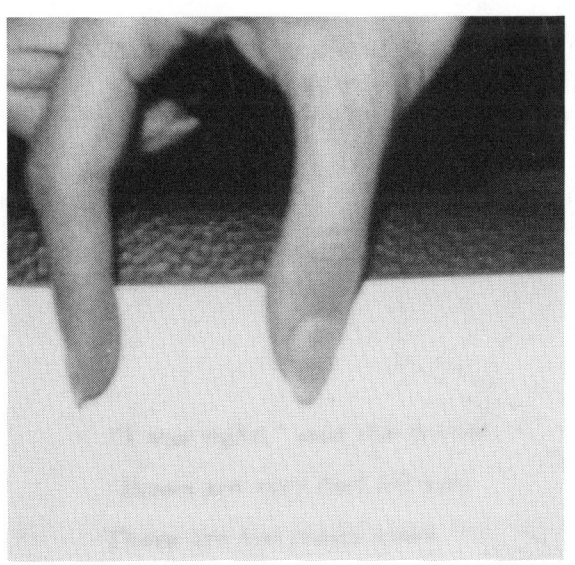

For Students With Visual Problems: How to Phrase the Words Visually

Students with visual problems often cannot keep their place on a page, or they may have difficulty focusing on the words. Sometimes youngsters reverse letters or words. To help these students when they read back a passage, it is best to focus their attention on phrases instead of individual words. Focusing can be accomplished by surrounding each phrase with your thumb and index finger, forming a semicircle slightly above the phrase to be read. This visual phrasing reinforces the auditory phrasing on the recording and helps to lessen reversals and word-by-word readings. As the youngster's fluency increases, this procedure may be discontinued.

How to Record Books on a 3^1 Level or Lower

When recording an easy storybook, the entire book can be recorded. Record about two to five minutes per tape side. Some very easy books may take only two tape sides (one tape cassette), while longer books may take many tape sides (perhaps 10 or more).

How to Record Books on a 3^2 Level or Higher

Higher level books are usually too long to record in their entirety. Using this recorded book method, a sixth grade book of 154 pages could take 50 or 100 tape cassettes. Unless the students are extremely fond of a particular book, it is much better to record articles, short stories, or chapters which represent highlights.

Training Volunteers to Record

Anyone who will record reading materials for students should read well and should have good diction and expression. The person training the volunteers will need to make sample tapes, or at least demonstrate the correct recording procedures. The proper phrasing and pacing need to be modeled thoroughly for volunteers, and the volunteers need to be given ample time to practice with the help of the trainer. Determine the amount per tape side so that there is a pattern that is easy for the volunteers to follow.

The tape cassette that accompanies this book contains model recordings of the passages in Chapter 5, and may be used in training volunteers.

How to Record For a Group

Most groups will have a wide range of reading abilities. When recording for a group of students, add a few months to the lowest reading level in the group and about 1 ½ years to the highest level. Then record books within that range. For example, suppose a second grade has reading levels that range from 1.0 to 4.0. Then books ranging from a 1.2 to a 5.5 level should be recorded for the youngsters in the group. For reinforcement purposes, a few 1.0 level books also might be recorded.

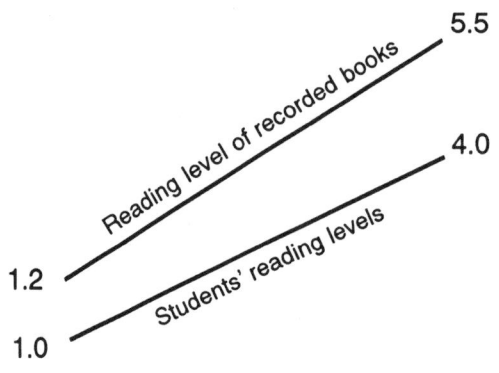

To begin, select a few passages, such as short stories or magazine articles, that are of great interest to the students. Then organize the reading materials by reading level or by subject. For older students, organizing by subject has been most effective because many youngsters feel embarrassed about reading easy books.

Next, decide how much to record on each tape side, write down the pages, code the tapes with an indelible marking pen, and start recording. Use the recording procedures at the end of this chapter, and the organization tips in Chapter 6.

Since the poorer readers may want to sample books as much as three to four years above their reading level, at least some of the more difficult books should be recorded in short segments (about three to four minutes per tape side), and the passage should be recorded at a somewhat slow pace. That way, poor readers can try some difficult books, and good readers can simply do more than one tape side at a sitting, if they are able.

A library of recorded books can be accumulated, if permanent recordings are made. In addition, a permanent library of tapes allows for the coordination of supplementary materials, such as the activity cards, games, audio cards, and reading skills exercises, described in Appendix A.

How to Record For One Student

The recorded book method has produced the highest gains when special recordings were made for individual students. Some youngsters have advanced a few years in reading ability in several months. For youngsters with *extreme* reading problems, individualized tape recordings may be assigned for about two to six months. After that period of time, most students will be ready for book tapes that have been recorded for a group.

One of the great advantages of making an individualized recording for a student is that the student's interests can be accommodated, and the pacing and phrasing can be synchronized with the youngster's reading and language-comprehension levels. A semi-permanent library of tapes can be accumulated so that the student can use the tapes in school or at home. These tapes can be changed every few weeks or months. An alternative approach is to use just one or two tape cassettes which contain the youngster's name on the spine. As the student masters a tape side, it is erased, and the next segment of the text is recorded.

Another important advantage of recordings made especially for one student is that the recording can be personalized. For example, a recording might begin like this: "Adam, we're going to continue with the story about Helen Keller that you enjoyed so much yesterday. If you recall, Helen had just met Annie Sullivan. Now, Adam, let's find out what Annie's plan is for helping Helen. Please turn to page 16."

The tape cassette that accompanies this book contains sample passages that were recorded for individual students, and some passages recorded for groups. (See Chapter 5 for more information.)

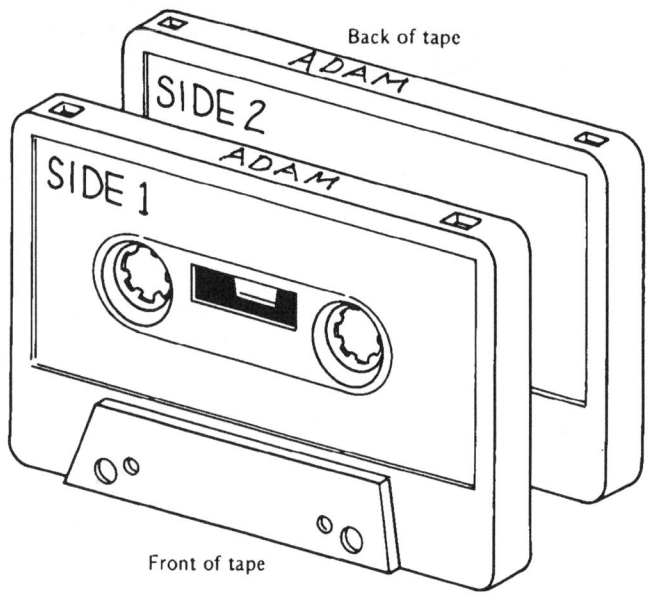

Figure 3-C. When recording for one youngster, code the tape cassette by writing the student's name on the spine of the cassette, and numbering each tape side.

How to Record For Older Students and Adults

The text should be recorded in small, sequential amounts. Usually older students like to read a larger amount of a story than younger children. For most students in sixth grade or higher, a five- to ten-minute recording has proven effective. If that is too much text for a youngster, simply have the student read along with the entire tape recording once, and re-listen to a small portion of the beginning of the recording a few times. By reducing the amount that must be mastered, the task becomes manageable for most students.

Storytell–Record–Storytell–Record

In addition to recording short stories, articles, and book chapters, another effective technique, which I call "storytell-record-storytell-record," involves alternating story telling with reading the story. For example, suppose a teacher wants to record Chapters 4 and

7 in a ten-chapter book. The first tape cassette could provide a summary of the story through the end of Chapter 3. The next few cassettes would contain the word-for-word readings of Chapter 4. A small portion of Chapter 4 is placed on each tape cassette in sequence. Chapters 5 and 6 would be summarized on the next tape cassette, and subsequent cassettes would contain the word-for-word recordings of Chapter 7. The last cassette would describe how the story ended.

Recording Very Small Amounts of Text Can Produce Large Reading Gains

Some older students have progressed at a rapid pace by reading very difficult books that have been recorded in extremely small amounts. During my first experimental trial with the recorded book method, the student who made the most progress was Tommy, a sixth grader reading on a first-grade level. Tommy asked me to record *Charlotte's Web* for him, which is a fifth-grade level book. I decided to record a highlight of the book (the chapter when Wilbur and Charlotte meet), and I recorded only a half-page per tape side, at a fairly slow pace. Tommy listened to my first recording five times, read it silently to himself, and then read the passage back to me smoothly. His reading was flawless! He paused in all the right places, read in phrases, and made no errors. Tommy and I worked for about 15-20 minutes daily, and in just six weeks, he gained 1.3 years in word recognition! Chapter 7 contains additional ideas for working with book tapes with secondary students and adults.

Step-By-Step: How to Record the Books

These are suggested procedures for recording books for maximum reading gains.

1. Set aside a block of quiet time to record. If necessary, inform people that you are recording and need quiet, and take the phone off the hook.

2. Decide which pages you will record on each tape cassette side, and code the tapes accordingly. (See coding techniques in Chapter 6.)

3. Turn on the tape recorder. Since every tape cassette has about 5 to 8 seconds of "lead time," let the tape run for about that amount of time before starting to record.

4. Speak into the microphone from a distance of approximately six to eight inches. If you hear little "explosions," on sounds such as "b," or "f," then your lips may be too close to the microphone. If your voice sounds too soft, you may be recording at too great a distance from the microphone.

5. In general, use the same naturally expressive voice you would use if you were reading to one child. If you are recording a book well above a youngster's or a group's reading level, exaggerate your expression slightly. *Above all, be natural, relaxed, and enjoy recording the story.*

6. Convey your interest in the book through your voice. Let the child feel your pleasure and enthusiasm.

7. Begin by reading the story title, providing a brief introduction, pausing, and then telling students the page to which they should turn. Pause long enough so that the youngster has enough time to turn pages and look at pictures.

8. End each tape with a cue that lets the listener know the recording is finished, such as, "Please rewind the tape for the next listener. That ends this recording." Without that important cue, some youngsters may listen to the blank tape for a while without realizing that the recording is finished.

9. Tell the student when to turn the page. As you begin each story, say, "Turn to page_____." Slowly reduce the cues until you need only pause, state the page number, and pause again. It is important to omit words from the cue gradually. "Turn to page...," may distract the listener from the story.

10. Since the story is all-important, when giving cues to the student, minimize the distraction by softening your voice.

11. Read the story in logical phrases, slowly enough so that most students can follow along, but not so slowly that they become bored. It is the way in which you phrase that will help to increase the student's reading comprehension.

12. Isolate unfamiliar words by pausing slightly before and after saying them. That will give youngsters more time to look at, absorb, and retain those words.

13. For those students with visual perception problems who lose their place easily on the page, teach them to follow the recording by placing a finger underneath the words they hear. Encourage the use of index cards as soon as possible.

Materials and Equipment Needed

Before beginning, you will need the following:

1. **Blank tape cassettes** — 15 minutes per tape side. The cassettes should be light in color so that they can be labeled and color coded, if necessary. A good source for inexpensive tape cassettes is Long's Electronics, 2704 Crestwood Blvd., Birmingham, AL 35210, 1-800-633-6461. Order C-32.

2. **Tape players.** Tape players usually are less expensive than tape recorders, and help to prevent accidental erasing of material that has been recorded on a cassette. If you have a listening center, only one tape player is needed. It is wise to have a spare tape player available. If a listening center will not be used, then at least 2 to 5 tape players with headsets, should be available for use by the students.

3. **Reading Materials.** There should be a wide variety of these for recording that are of great interest to the students. (See Chapter 4 and Appendix D.)

Chapter 4

How to Select the Books

The Goal: To Turn Unmotivated Readers Into Avid Readers

Most poor readers are extremely unmotivated about reading, or anything having to do with the act of reading. They don't want to read, many do not complete reading assignments, and they seldom, if ever, read voluntarily. Teachers who have used the recorded book method have noted repeatedly that students who formerly *hated* reading, begin to *love* it. There are at least two reasons why this happens. First, the recordings usually enable students to read immediately, with ease and fluency, material that is well above their reading level. Confidence builds quickly. The second reason is also important. Many students for the first time in their school career, can read something that they find genuinely interesting.

Four Factors That Should Affect Book Selection

When books are recorded for students, these four important factors should determine which books are recorded: the quality of the writing; the student's language-comprehension level; the student's reading level; and the student's interests (Carbo, 1984).

1. Quality of the Writing

Many book publishers list books of high quality among their offerings. Librarians and lists of award-winning books are two excellent resources. (Also see Appendix D for lists of recommended books to record.) To determine the quality of the reading material, the following checklist may be helpful.

INDICATORS OF GOOD WRITING

☐ 1. Does the author capture the interest of the reader almost immediately?
☐ 2. Will the reader want to read on? Is there a clear purpose for reading?
☐ 3. If the book is fictional, does it create an air of expectancy, suspense, mystery?
☐ 4. Is the book at least one of these? (a) entertaining, (b) informative, (c) exciting, (d) humorous?
☐ 5. Is rich and imaginative language used?

☐ 6. Does the writer have good command of the language?
☐ 7. Do the sentences vary in structure and length?
☐ 8. Is original and evocative imagery used?

2. The Student's Language-Comprehension Level

When selecting books to record, the student's language-comprehension level is a powerful factor. (By "language-comprehension level," I mean the level of spoken language a youngster can comprehend.) For example, let us suppose that you were choosing books to record for two youngsters who have average intelligence, average language-comprehension abilities, and who read on a fourth-grade level. The main difference between them is that Jennifer is in fifth grade while Bruce is in ninth grade. A more difficult book should be recorded for Bruce who is interested in, and capable of understanding, ninth-grade level vocabulary and concepts.

Bruce's fourth-grade reading level, however, would probably make it unwise to start with a ninth-grade book. Because Bruce's language-comprehension level is five years higher than his reading level, it would be advisable to begin recording sixth- or even seventh-grade level books for him. In Jennifer's case, since her language-comprehension and reading levels differ by only one year, books approximately six months to one year above her reading level should be recorded for her. As quickly as possible, each student should move on to more difficult books.

3. The Student's Reading Level

When selecting books to record for students, consider whether they read above or below a second-grade reading level. Generally, those who read below that level will need books closer to their reading level, than will those who read above it. Nonreaders usually require reading materials that are very simple and contain few words which are repeated often. The following three categories are offered as a guide for book selection.

- *Students who have attained at least a second-grade reading level.* For the youngsters whose language-comprehension level is about two or more years higher than their reading level, try recording books that are about one to 1 ½ years above their reading level. If the reading and language comprehension levels are similar, or if there is a small difference, record books that are about six months above the student's reading level.
- *Students who read below a second-grade level.* For these youngsters, record books that are about six months above their reading level, provided that their level of comprehension is at least as high as the book. If not, then record books that are just a few months above the student's reading level.
- *Nonreaders.* Generally, young children who are not able to read should begin with very simple storybooks, or pre-primers. For older students who are nonreaders, pre-primers usually will embarrass or insult them. In those cases it may be more effective to begin with stories

created by the student. Either ask them to dictate short stories and then record them, or ask the youngsters to dictate their stories directly into a tape recorder. Then a teacher or aide can write down what the student recorded. To organize the students' own tape recorded stories, tape or paste the story inside a folder, and label the folder and tape cassette (see Figure 4-A). Also record simple storybooks that have (a) interesting, descriptive pictures (to provide a strong context for the student), (b) only about five to ten words on each page (so that the child is not overwhelmed with words to learn), and (c) words repeated sufficiently so that the child can commit them to memory.

4. The Student's Interests

For this method to be most effective, the reading materials should be extremely interesting to a student. In the case of poor readers who have generally grown to dislike reading, high-interest reading materials are crucial. Since virtually *any* reading material can be recorded, it makes good sense to record only what the student is most likely to enjoy.

When conducting my initial experiments with the recorded book method, I found that students made the greatest progress with recordings of high-interest storybooks, rather than with recordings of the basal reader. For youngsters who read on a 1^2 level or above, the most rapid gains were made when I recorded books that were close to their language-comprehension level, which usually was much higher than their reading level. The students learned and retained words more easily and permanently when the words were imbedded within contexts that interested them. On the other hand, they had difficulty recalling isolated words, or words presented in dull contexts. The reader's interests are very important. Yet, throughout the grades, more often than not, youngsters are *told* what to read. Seldom are they given choices.

The *Reading Interest Inventory*™, on the next page, can be used as a guide for determining students' interests. This inventory can be added to, and adapted to the age-level of the students.

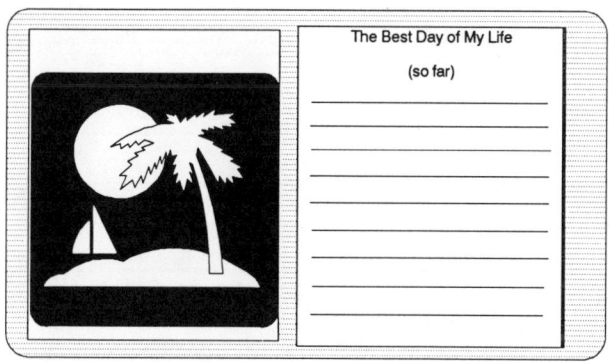 

Figure 4-A. This technique is especially good for older students who are nonreaders or who read well below their grade level. Affix the student's own story inside a folder. Record the story on one or two tape sides using the procedures outlined in Chapter 3. Then label the folder and the tape cassette.

Reading Interest Inventory™

Name_____

Grade Level_____ Date_____

Place an "X" on each line to indicate how interested you are in each topic.

　　　　　　　　　　　_____

　　　　　　　　　not interested　　　　　　　　　　very interested

1. I like to read books with:

adventure	_____
animals	_____
biographies	_____
children	_____
countries	_____
fairy tales	_____
families	_____
fantasy	_____
folk tales	_____
history	_____
humor	_____
jokes and riddles	_____
mystery	_____
mythology	_____
pets	_____
romance	_____
scary stories	_____
school	_____
science	_____
science fiction	_____
sports	_____

Other things I like to read about are: _____

_____

_____

Reading Interest Inventory™ - Page 2

2. *I like to read:*

　　☐ books with facts
　　☐ comic books
　　☐ magazines
　　☐ newspapers
　　☐ plays
　　☐ poems
　　☐ short stories
　　☐ storybooks

Other kinds of things that I like to read are:
_____
_____
_____
_____
_____

3. *I am interested in:*

　　☐ baseball
　　☐ boats
　　☐ cars
　　☐ chess
　　☐ dancing
　　☐ dolls
　　☐ football
　　☐ hockey
　　☐ karate
　　☐ kites
　　☐ machinery
　　☐ motorcycles
　　☐ music
　　☐ sewing
　　☐ soccer

Other things that I am interested in are:
_____
_____
_____
_____
_____

Reading Interest Inventory™ - Page 3

4. Some kinds of books and stories I think I would like to read are:

_____

_____

5. Some books and stories that I've liked are:

_____

_____

_____

6. Some things that I like to do when I have free time are:

_____

_____

_____

7. Some of my favorite movies are:

_____

_____

_____

8. My favorite T.V. shows are:

_____

_____

_____

9. Some favorite people that I really like are:

_____

_____

_____

10. My favorite animals are:

_____

_____

_____

How to Record a Basal Reader Versus a Storybook

As a general rule, books that contain a highly-controlled vocabulary, and which introduce new words very gradually, may be recorded in larger amounts on each tape side, than books that have a less controlled vocabulary and introduce new words rapidly. For students who are unable to handle books that introduce many words quickly, record just a few minutes, and provide ample practice of the vocabulary (see Appendix A).

How to Select Books for Young, Beginning Readers

The books that are most easily mastered by this group are usually those that contain repetitive vocabulary within a high-interest context. In an excellent article by Lauritzen (1980), these four, specific linguistic patterns used in folk tales were described as helping young children to read a storybook with ease.

1. Repeated Wording. Uses sets of words like a chorus, such as "Clementine," "Skip to My Lou," "Oh, Susanna," and this excerpt from "Millions of Cats":

> Hundreds of cats
> Thousands of cats
> Millions and billions
> and trillions of cats.
>   (W. Gag, 1929)

2. Repeated Syntax Patterns. New words are inserted into a syntactic structure that is repeated many times, such as "This Old Man," "Ninety-nine Bottles of Beer," or this story by Barchas (1975), *I Was Walking Down the Road.*

> I was walking down the road.
> Then I saw a little toad.
> I caught it.
> I picked it up.
> I put it in a cage.
>
> I was looking at the sky.
> Then I saw a butterfly.
> I caught it.
> I picked it up.
> I put it in a cage.
>   (Barchas, 1975)

3. Link Wording. Repeats the words or phrases at the end of a sentence, such as "The Farmer in the Dell," or:

> Obadiah jumped in a fire.
> The *fire* was so hot, he jumped in a *pot*.
> The *pot* was so black, he jumped in a *crack*.
> The *crack* was so high, he jumped to the *sky*.
> The sky...

4. Cumulative Structure. Repeats episodes rather than words. One example is the story, "The House That Jack Built." A memory game that children play also uses cumulative structure. In this game, the first child might say, "I'm going to the store and I will buy apricots." The second child repeats this sentence and adds an item beginning with the letter "b." This child might say, "I'm going to the store and I will buy apricots and bananas." This process continues through the entire alphabet.

Courtesy, Robert W. Carbonaro School, Valley Stream, NY.

A Word About Whole-Language Programs

For many children in whole-language programs, use of the recorded book method will speed up their progress considerably. Good readers usually can improve their fluency with the aid of commercial recordings of stories, while poor to average readers often benefit from slower recordings.

While many students will do extremely well in a whole-language approach, there may be some who will not. To succeed easily in a whole-language program, youngsters must have visual, tactile and global strengths. Children who are not strong visually, may be helped with phonics, if they are sufficiently auditory and analytic. Children who have low visual *and* low auditory abilities probably will need a great deal of repetition– especially through their tactile and kinesthetic modalities – before a word becomes a sight word.

One difficulty with whole-language materials may occur at the beginning reading levels. Books in whole-language programs usually have a greater range of vocabulary than do those in a basal reader series. While the books in a whole-language program are often interesting and well written (and this is *very* important), they can present a problem for youngsters who need to see and experience a word many times before it becomes a sight word.

Books with repetitious vocabulary can be of great help to such youngsters. But for some, even the predictable books with repeated vocabulary still do not provide enough practice of the small vocabulary. These children may benefit from the controlled vocabulary of a basal, but the boredom that can result if the stories are uninteresting makes it difficult for the youngster to learn the words. Word retention is usually increased when the learner is interested in the book. There is no easy answer to this dilemma.

If the decision is made to record pre-primers with highly-controlled vocabularies, then as soon as the child has mastered about 20 to 25 words, simple storybooks should also be recorded. For those with memory difficulties, record the books in short segments (perhaps one-minute recordings), few words per phrase (only one to three), permit many repetitions of the recording (as many as five), and provide a great deal of supplementary practice of the words in the recorded passage, before moving on to the next segment of the story. (Appendix A describes some of the techniques for practicing words.)

Courtesy, The Key School, New York City Public Schools, New York, NY.

Chapter 5

Sample Recordings For Groups and Individual Students

This chapter contains ten sample passages that have been recorded on the tape cassette that accompanies this book. Each passage illustrates the appropriate pace, phrasing and expression. The first tape side contains samples 1-6 for Grades 1-3, and tape side 2 has samples 7-10 for Grades 4 through adult.

As mentioned previously, the recorded book method has produced the highest gains when special recordings were made for individual students. Some few youngsters have gained two years in just two months. I would advise special, individual recordings for any youngsters who are experiencing severe reading problems. The tape recording takes only a few minutes to make, and the benefits usually are immediate and lasting, provided that the tape cassettes are used often and consistently. While recordings made for groups of students are generally not as effective as those made for individuals, many youngsters have made excellent reading gains with group recordings.

The 10 excerpts that follow provide a good model for recording. The pacing and phrasing of the passages on the sample recordings do not represent *the only* correct strategies. Rather, they are offered as guidelines for those who would like to learn the technique.

On some recordings, for example, the listener is instructed to, "Put your finger under the words as you hear them." This is done so that the child learns to track the words and so that the teacher can observe whether or not the student is both listening to *and* looking at the words. This direction can be eliminated from the tape recording, but I would advise that a student be instructed to "trace your finger under the words as you hear them," the first few times he or she listens to a recording.

Notice that the cue for directing the student to move on to the next page is the actual page number. This procedure helps most students to keep their place and has been more effective than using a sound effect like a bell. The page cue should be shortened quickly, and it should be said very quietly so it distracts the listener from the story as little as possible.

In the sample passages that follow, the sweeping lines under the words indicate the phrasing that was used on the recording. It is perfectly fine to phrase differently than these recordings, as long as the phrasing conveys the printed message correctly. The student is to look at the pages containing the story while listening to the recording. The story pages do not have any sweeping lines drawn in.

A good way to learn how to record books for maximum reading gains, is to listen to these samples. Then record some books and use them with students. Observe the youngsters and ask them whether the recordings are too fast, too slow, etc. Adjust your recordings accordingly. Here, now, are 10 model recordings.

Note: RL=Reading Level; LCL=Language-Comprehension Level; Gap=difference between RL of book and RL of student; WPM=words per minute; PP=Pre-Primer

Figure 5-A. Page 3 of Teddy Bear, Teddy Bear, *illustrated by Sheila Somerville. A Nellie Edge I CAN READ BOOK.*

Model 1: How to Record For Jeremy, Grade 1

Late in October, Jeremy entered first grade from another school. He was a total nonreader. It is mid-November and Jeremy has just finished a pre-primer, has a sight vocabulary of about 20 words, and is ready for some simple storybooks like this big book, *Teddy Bear, Teddy Bear* (available from Nellie Edge, see Appendix D). The book is the first of a series of easy books specially recorded for Jeremy. There are four tape sides to this book. The excerpt below is from the first tape side of the first book in the series. (Note: If the child's name is not mentioned on the recording, then the recording is reusable with other youngsters.)

On the next page, there is a sample recording of a story from the book *Mouse Tales,* which was made for Jeremy's class. "The Bath" passage is difficult for Jeremy, and is recorded at too-fast a pace for him. But Jeremy can use *Mouse Tales* and the tapes for enjoyment. And, if Jeremy is instructed to listen to the whole tape recording once, and then re-listen 3 or 4 times to *only a small portion* of the beginning (perhaps only a half-page), he probably will remember some of the words.

> Jeremy: Grade 1; RL: PP; LCL: Average
> Book: *Teddy Bear, Teddy Bear*
> Reading Level of Book: About P
> Gap: A few months
> How to Record:
>   PACE: Very slow, about 40 WPM
>   PHRASING: Very short phrases, about 1-2 words per phrase
>   EXPRESSION: Slightly exaggerated
>   LENGTH: About 1 ½ to 2 minutes

Teddy Bear, Teddy Bear

Jeremy, I'm very proud of how well you're reading. This is Book 1, Tape Side 1. This story is called *Teddy Bear, Teddy Bear.* And that's what the words say on the cover of the book. Put your finger under those words, *Teddy Bear, Teddy Bear.* Good. As you listen, imagine yourself jumping rope, and doing all the things that Teddy Bear does.

Please open your book now, Jeremy, to page 1 (pause). Put your finger under the words as you hear them (pause). Page 1.

> *Teddy Bear, Teddy Bear, turn around (pause).*
>
> *Page 2 (pause)*
>
> *Teddy Bear, Teddy Bear, touch the ground (pause).*
>
> *3 (pause)*
>
> *Teddy Bear, Teddy Bear, show your shoe (pause).*
>
> *4 (pause)*
>
> *Teddy Bear, Teddy Bear, I love you.*

Jeremy, we'll find out more things that Teddy Bear can do on the next tape side. Please rewind this tape. Listen to it again if you want to. When you're ready, read the story back to me. That ends this recording.

There was once a mouse

who was dirty,

so he took a bath.

The water

filled up the bathtub.

Figure 5-b. Page 55 from Mouse Tales, *written and illustrated by Arnold Lobel.*

Model 2: How to Record For Jeremy's First-Grade Class

By November of first grade, the children in Jeremy's class have listened to and read many predictable books. Most are ready for this charming story, "The Bath," one of 7 stories in the book, *Mouse Tales*. The entire story (7 pages), could be placed on one tape side. If that is done, then the better readers would listen one to three times to the entire story, while the slower readers, like Jeremy, would listen to the entire story once, and then re-listen to a small portion (i.e., the first page or two). Subsequently, the slower readers could increase the amount of text that they listen to repeatedly and master (i.e., the first 3 or 4 pages), until, finally, they may be able to read the entire story with fluency. Youngsters should be encouraged to achieve mastery of difficult books only if they are strongly motivated. After using many special recordings of books such as *Mouse Tales*, many students will be ready for commercial recordings, which usually have more text per tape side, and are recorded at a faster pace.

> Grade 1 Students: RL: P to 2.0; LCL: Average
> Story: "The Bath" from *Mouse Tales* by Arnold Lobel
> RL of Book: Grade 1
> Gap: From 0 to 1 year
> How to Record:
> > PACE: Somewhat slow, about 70 WPM
> > PHRASING: Short phrases, about 2-3 words per phrase
> > EXPRESSION: Fairly natural
> > LENGTH: About 3 minutes

"The Bath"

Tape Side 7, *Mouse Tales*. I'm going to read you the last story called, "The Bath." This one is my favorite. Please turn to page 55 (pause). Put your finger under the words as you hear them. (Pause) Page 55.

> *There was once a mouse who was dirty,*
>
> *so he took a bath.*
>
> *The water filled up the bathtub.*
>
> *Page 56 (pause).*
>
> *But the mouse was still dirty,*
>
> *so he let the water run over onto the floor.*
>
> *The water filled up the bathroom*
>
> *But the mouse was still dirty,*
>
> *57 (pause)*
>
> *so he let the water run out of the window.*
>
> *The water filled up the street.*
>
> *But the mouse was still dirty.*

Figure 5-C. From Bread and Jam For Frances, *illustrated by Lillian Hoban.*

Model 3: How to Record For Elena, Grade 2

Elena is a bright, bilingual second grader. Her English is somewhat limited. The recorded books are excellent for increasing both Elena's sight vocabulary and her speaking vocabulary. Elena has enjoyed listening to the Frances books, understands most of the words, and requested this recording. This book is number 10 in a series of easy books. The book, *Bread and Jam For Frances*, has been recorded on 7 tape sides for Elena. The excerpt below is about ½ of tape side 3, which has pages 14 to 17 recorded on it.

Elena: Grade 2^2; RL: 1.5; LCL: Below-Average in English
Book: *Bread and Jam For Frances* by Russell Hoban
RL of Book: 2.5 to 3.0
Gap: About one year
How to Record:
    PACE: Slow, about 65 WPM
    PHRASING: Short phrases, about 2-4 words per phrase
    EXPRESSION: Slightly exaggerated
    LENGTH: About 2 to 3 minutes

Bread and Jam For Frances

Bread and Jam For Frances, Book 10, Side 3. It looks like Frances just doesn't want to eat *anything* but bread and jam, bread and jam. Her parents have a plan. Let's find out what it is. Please turn to page 14 (pause). Put your finger under the words as you hear them. Page 14.

The next morning at breakfast, Father sat down

and said, "Now I call that a pretty sight!

Fresh orange juice and poached eggs on toast.

There's a proper breakfast for you!"

"Thank you for saying so," said Mother.

"Poached eggs on toast do have a cheery look, I think."

Frances began to sing a poached-egg song:

Poached eggs on toast, why do you shiver

With such a funny little quiver?

Then she looked down and saw

that she did not have a poached egg.

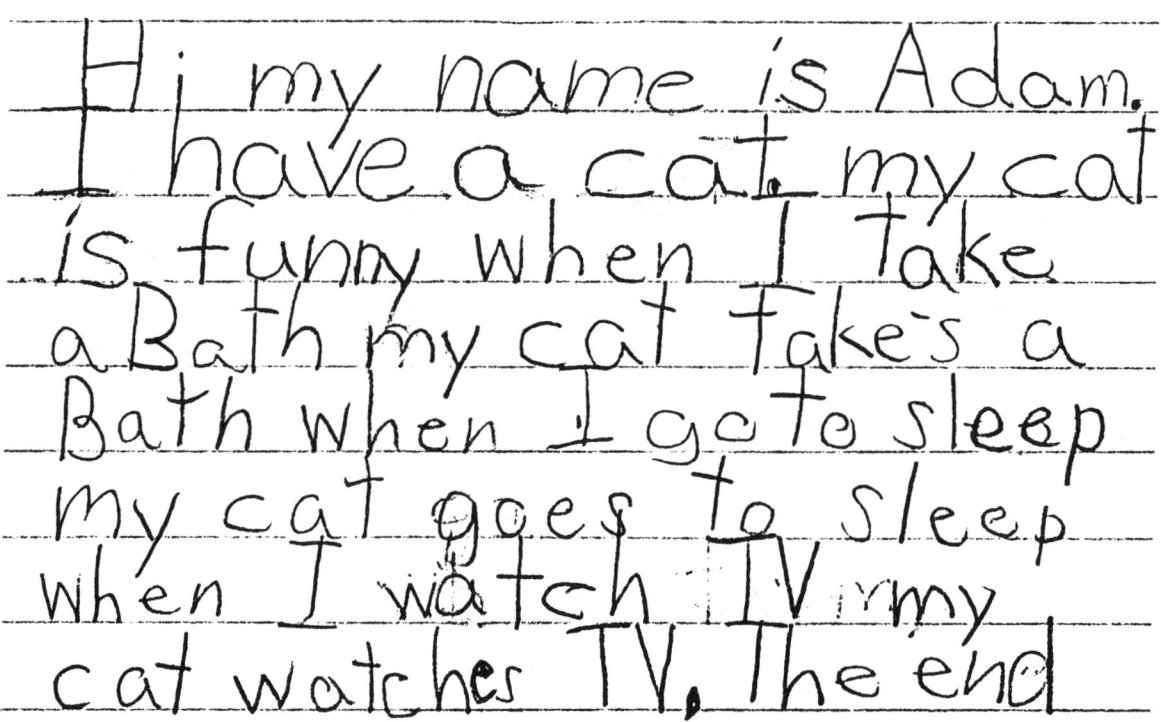

Figure 5-D. Although Adam was in the third grade, he was reading on a primer level. After listening to recordings of his own stories, like the one above, Adam's sight vocabulary increased substantially.

Model 4: How to Record for Adam, Grade 3

Adam finds it difficult to remember words unless he sees them many times. He has been ill a great deal, and has moved three times since he began school. As a result, Adam is reading haltingly on a pre-primer level.

One of Adam's favorite pastimes is to write and illustrate his own stories. Here is an excellent opportunity to combine two reading methods that match Adam's reading style: the recorded book method and the language-experience method. The excerpt below is from a story composed by Adam. After he finishes working with the recording, Adam will use audio cards and a game that provides more practice of the words in his story. (See Chapter 4 for organizing tape recordings of a student's own stories, and Appendix A for making the audio cards and games.)

>Adam: Grade 3; RL: PP; LCL: Average
>Book: Own story
>RL of Story: About Primer
>Gap: A few months
>How to Record:
>>PACE: Slow, about 50-55 WPM
>>PHRASING: Short phrases, about 1-3 words per phrase
>>EXPRESSION: Slightly exaggerated
>>LENGTH: About 2 minutes

"My Funny Cat"

Adam, I'd really like to see your funny cat. Here is your story about your cat. Please put your finger under the words as you hear me read your story.

>*My Funny Cat*
>
>*Hi, my name is Adam.*
>
>*I have a cat.*
>
>*My cat is funny.*
>
>*When I take a bath,*
>
>*my cat takes a bath.*
>
>*When I go to sleep,*
>
>*my cat goes to sleep.*
>
>*When I watch T.V.,*
>
>*my cat watches T.V.*
>
>*The end.*

Adam, it sounds like your cat loves you very much. Please rewind the tape. That ends this recording.

Figure 5-E. From The Emperor's New Clothes, *told and illustrated by Val Biro.*

Model 5: How to Record For an Average Third-Grade Class

For any group, record books that range in reading level, from *slightly above* the lowest to *above* the highest in the class. Two sample recordings follow. The first, an excerpt from *The Emperor's New Clothes*, is written on a beginning third-grade level. The second passage from the story, "The Visitor from Heaven," is written on a sixth-grade level. The reading levels of the two passages differ markedly, but both stories are not above the language-comprehension levels of most of the children in this group. Notice how differently each passage is recorded. The easier story is recorded at a faster pace, in larger amounts, and in longer phrases than the more difficult one. Both stories are part of a series of fantasy stories that will be recorded. *The Emperor's New Clothes* is the first book in the series, while "The Visitor from Heaven" is the tenth.

Grade 3 Students: RL: 2.0 to 4.5; LCL: Average
Book: *The Emperor's New Clothes* by Val Biro
RL of Book: Approximately 3.0
Gap: 0 to 1 year
How to Record:
  PACE: Almost natural, about 85-90 WPM
  PHRASING: Long phrases, about 2-6 words per phrase
  EXPRESSION: Natural
  LENGTH: About 4 minutes

(What follows is the last part of the recording...)

The Emperor's New Clothes

But suddenly a small child looked at the Emperor and cried,

"He's got nothing on at all!"

23 *(pause)*

Everyone heard. They looked at the Emperor. Then they looked at each other and looked at the Emperor again.

At last all the people shouted,

"He's got nothing on at all!"

24 *(pause)*

The Emperor blushed. He knew that they were right.

But he walked bravely on, pink from head to toe.

And that ends the story of *The Emperor's New Clothes*. What lesson do you think the Emperor may have learned in this story? Tell me in a note. Please rewind this tape. That ends this recording.

Figure 5-F. From "The Visitor From Heaven," illustrated by Beverly Curl.

Model 6: Another Recording for an Average Third-Grade Class

Grade 3 Students: RL: 2.0 to 4.5; LCL: Average
Story: "The Visitor From Heaven" by Beulah Candappa
RL of Book: Approximately 6.0
Gap: 1 ½ to 4 years
How to Record:
    PACE: Slow, about 80 WPM
    PHRASING: Short phrases, 2-5 words per phrase
    EXPRESSION: Slightly exaggerated
    LENGTH: About 2 to 3 minutes
(Side 1 of this cassette discussed the map on the inside cover of the book.)

"The Visitor from Heaven"

Book 10, Side 2, *Tales of South Asia: Legendary Creatures*. Look at the map on the inside cover of the book. Today's story comes from the country of Sri Lanka. It is a tiny country south of India. Say it with me, very quietly, "Sri Lanka." Good. Now turn to page 4, relax, and enjoy this story with me. The story is called, "The Visitor from Heaven." Put your finger under the words as you hear them. Page 4.

Many religions say it is difficult for a rich man to enter heaven. This story from Sri Lanka is about one man who tried to get there on the back of a heavenly visitor.

There was once a rich landlord who was mean, and because he was so mean, he would not sleep at night.

"What?" he shouted, when his wife reminded him that he should go to sleep, "Waste all that time **sleeping** *when I could be making more money? Nonsense!" So he stayed awake all night tossing and turning in his bed, keeping his wife awake, and scheming...how to make more money....Every morning the landlord visited his paddy fields to make sure his rice plants were flourishing; also to see that no damage had been done by straying cattle or wild animals during the night.*

Figure 5-G. From Amelia Bedelia, *illustrated by Fritz Siebel.*

Model 7: How to Record For Mary, Grade 4

Mary is reading 2 years below grade level. She loves funny, silly stories, and *Amelia Bedelia* is one of her favorites. After a month or two of using tape recordings of simple stories that are fairly close to her language-comprehension level every day in school and at home, Mary's sight vocabulary should improve sufficiently so that she can move up to more difficult third- and then fourth-grade level books. This is an excerpt of the first tape side of *Amelia Bedelia* as recorded for Mary.

Mary: Grade 4; RL:2.0; LCL: Average
Book: *Amelia Bedelia* by Peggy Parish
RL of the Book: About 2.0 to 2.5
Gap: About 3 to 5 months
How to Record:
    PACE: Fairly slow, about 65 WPM
    PHRASING: Short phrases, about 2-4 words per phrase
    EXPRESSION: Slightly exaggerated
    LENGTH: About 3 minutes

Amelia Bedelia

Book 7, Side 3, *Amelia Bedelia*. Amelia Bedelia is a very, very silly maid. She's cut up some towels and put dusting powder all over the furniture. Let's find out more silly things that she does. Please turn to page 11. Put your finger under the words as you hear them. Page 11.

Draw the drapes when the sun comes in.

read Amelia Bedelia.

She looked up.

The sun was coming in.

Amelia Bedelia looked at the list again.

"Draw the drapes?

That's what it says.

I'm not much of a hand at drawing, but I'll try."

Page 12

So Amelia Bedelia sat right down and she drew those drapes.

Gorbachev Says Change Will Sweep Bloc

By JAMES M. MARKHAM
Special to The New York Times

PARIS, July 5 — President Mikhail S. Gorbachev said today that Poles and Hungarians were free to determine their political future but predicted that Communist countries now in transition would find "a new quality of life within a socialist system, a socialist democracy."

At a lively news conference with President François Mitterrand at the Elysée Palace, the Soviet President was asked about the possibility that swift political change in Poland and Hungary could leave their Communist parties out of power.

"How the Polish people and the Hungarian people will decide to structure their societies and lives will be their affair," Mr. Gorbachev said. But he predicted that "the process of democratization" would ultimately transform not just Poland and Hungary but all of Eastern Europe.

Polish and Hungarian political leaders say Mr. Gorbachev has repeatedly told them in closed-door talks that they are free to change their political institutions and economic policies without having to fear Soviet interference, and he has made general statements in public about encouraging greater independence among Communist countries. But Mr. Gorbachev is not thought to have been so explicit on this delicate topic in public.

Possible Meeting With Walesa

In response to another question, Mr. Gorbachev said he saw no obstacle to meeting with Lech Walesa, the leader of the Solidarity movement, whose forces scored a stunning success in Poland's general elections last month.

The Soviet President also praised Gen. Wojciech Jaruzelski, who has decided not to run for the Polish presidency after the electoral drubbing suffered by the Communist Party, as "a great politician and a man of high moral responsibility."

Asked if his innovative course would survive if he disappeared from the scene, Mr. Gorbachev said his policies did "not have to be tied to Gorbachev himself."

"Why the concern?" he asked the journalist who asked the question. "Are you worried about my health? Do you have some terrible news?"

Responding to another question, Mr. Gorbachev revealed that he had been baptized and christened, which he described as "quite normal" in the Soviet Union. He said the rehabilitation of Aleksandr Solzhenitsyn, the exiled Russian author whose "Gulag Archipelago" is being published in the Soviet Union, was "a practical matter, and will be resolved in a practical manner."

'Second Wind' for Socialism

Mr. Gorbachev challenged the assertion that Communism was in crisis around the world, and wove through his remarks caveats about the dangers of "destabilization" of perestroika, his program of political and economic restructuring.

"To say that we have rejected socialism is simply misleading," he said. "If we can bring people back into the socialist system instead of alienating them, we can give socialism a second wind."

At the end of two days of talks, Mr. Mitterrand and Mr. Gorbachev issued an unusual joint appeal for an immediate cease-fire in Lebanon, calling for an end to the arming of Lebanese factions and respect for the battered nation's sovereignty.

The text did not mention Syria, which occupies much of Lebanon and is armed by the Soviet Union, or Iraq, which also is armed by Moscow and supplies the Lebanese Christian forces challenging Syria.

Caution on Capitalism

Earlier in the day, the Soviet President cautioned that the creation of "a common European home" reaching from the Urals to the Atlantic could not come about through the rollback of socialism in Eastern Europe.

Speaking to professors, writers and students at the Sorbonne, the Soviet President warned the West against expecting that Eastern Europe would "return to the capitalist fold" and "cultivating the illusion that only bourgeois society represents eternal values."

"This is not the way to follow if one wants to arrive at a consensus on the common European home," Mr. Gorbachev said. "Some would like to see the problem of Europe solved by the displacement of socialism, but I think this is unreal and even dangerous."

The Soviet leader has made the "common European home" the theme of his visit to France, and he is expected to elaborate on it when he addresses the Council of Europe in Strasbourg on Thursday before flying to Rumania for a meeting of the Warsaw Pact.

Mr. Gorbachev's appearance at the Sorbonne appeared to have been intended to woo French intellectuals, who have in many instances been in the forefront of the criticism of totalitarian systems. But he disappointed many in the audience by failing to condemn the violent repression of the democracy movement in China.

"We cannot interfere directly and give advice," said Mr. Gorbachev, who asserted that a period of "calming down" had begun in China. "We would like to see the Chinese people succeed, to see a peaceful China reintegrated in the world."

Figure 5-H. Article titled, "Gorbachev Says Change Will Sweep Bloc," by James M. Markham, from The New York Times *International, July 6, 1989, p. A-3.*

Model 8: How to Record for an Above-Average, Sixth-Grade Class

This sixth grade has been studying the history of Russia. Their teacher has recorded a series of articles about Russia. Each article has been stapled inside a separate folder, with multiple copies of the article also placed inside the folder. Each tape cassette is numbered to correspond with the folder containing the article.

The excerpt that follows is about 1/10 of the original article, which was recorded in its entirety. The students are familiar with the concepts, which have been discussed in class. These articles and recordings can be used as resources for report writing, and, if multiple copies of the tape cassettes are made, the youngsters can sign out cassettes and articles to use at home.

> Grade 6 Students: RL: 6.0 to 10.5; LCL: Above-average
> Article: "Gorbachev Says Change Will Sweep Bloc" by James M. Markham
> RL of Article: Approximately 15th Grade
> Gap: 4 to 9 years
> How to Record:
>   PACE: Fairly slow, about 85-95 WPM
>   PHRASING: About 3-6 words per phrase
>   EXPRESSION: Natural
>   LENGTH: About 5 minutes

"Gorbachev Says Change Will Sweep Bloc"

As we discussed in class, dramatic political changes are occurring in many communist countries. This article from the *New York Times* International section, is a summary of a speech delivered by President Mikhail Gorbachev in Paris. He discusses "perestroika," his program of restructuring the soviet bloc countries.

> *PARIS, July 5 - President Mikhail S. Gorbachev said today that Poles and Hungarians were free to determine their political future but predicted that Communist countries now in transition would find "a new quality of life within a socialist system, a socialist democracy."*
>
> *At a lively news conference with President François Mitterrand at the Elysée Palace, the Soviet President was asked about the possibility that swift political change in Poland and Hungary could leave their Communist parties out of power.*

Model 9: How to Record For High School Students With Reading Problems

Assume that a resource teacher is working with students in grades 9-12 with severe reading problems. Most of the youngsters are candidates for dropping out of school. They have short attention spans, seldom do their homework, are seldom prepared for tests, and have difficulty remembering most school work. An ideal book for this group would be, *I Hate School: How to Hang In and When to Drop Out*. It is candid, and offers step-by-step advice toward better study and homework habits. The book is divided into small chunks that are ideal for recording.

This recording will be used in a small-group setting, using the strategies outlined by Briggs and Sorrell in Chapter 7. Students attend the resource room in small groups. There are enough copies of *I Hate School*, so that every youngster has his/her own. A few of the students can read the book without the aid of the recording; others will use "Walkman-like" tape players at their desks. After the entire group reads the pages assigned (about one half-chapter), and discusses them, copies of the tape cassette will be made available for the students to take home and use. The slower readers will be instructed to listen to the entire tape once, and then re-listen two to three times to just the first page or two to improve their reading ability.

Since the main purpose of this recording is to impart content, a larger amount of the book has been recorded on each tape side than would have been recorded if the purpose were mainly to improve reading ability. That is why the pace is faster, and the phrases are longer than most of the other sample passages in this chapter. Here is a small portion of a 4-minute recording of this excellent book.

> Grade 9-12: RL: 2.2 to 6.4; LCL: Below-Average
> Book: *I Hate School: How to Hang In and When to Drop Out*
> by Claudine G. Wirths and Mary Bowman-Kruhm
> RL of Book: Approximately 6.4
> Gap: 0 to 4 years
> How to Record:
> > PACE: Fairly slow, about 90 WPM
> > PHRASING: About 3-8 words per phrase
> > EXPRESSION: Natural
> > LENGTH: About 4 minutes

I Hate School: How to Hang in and When to Drop Out

Book 14, Side 10. We're going to begin the sixth chapter titled, "Test-Taking Tricks." This chapter should help you to study better and feel less nervous about taking tests. We'll talk about the key ideas after you finish this tape recording. Please open the book to page 88 (pause). Put your finger under the words as you hear them. Page 88 (pause).

Chapter 6, Test-Taking Tricks (pause).

People have to take tests all through life. Teachers give tests to find out what kinds of grades to give you and also to find out what kinds of problems you are having. Employers give tests to find out what you are good at doing or whether you can do the job you are applying for. The Department of Motor Vehicles gives tests to find out whether you can be licensed to drive. You just have to get used to the idea of tests.

I hate taking tests. I get nervous and don't do well, even if I know the answers pretty well.

Taking a test makes even the best student nervous. What you need to do is turn that anxiety and the adrenaline it produces into a source of energy to help you do better. Let's talk about what you can do before the test and during it.

The stuff the teacher tells us seems so obvious that I figure I don't need to study until the night before the test.

What you are doing is **cramming.** *If you understand all the teacher tells you during class, that means you have a good teacher. You still need to go over the work at night to be able to remember it. But trying to learn everything in* **one** *night is asking your brain to do the impossible. The more you go over your studies, the more you will remember.*

Figure 5-K. A view of Hong Kong that reveals a strange mixture of an old and a new world.

Model 10: How to Record For Jonathan, Age 24

Jonathan is a bright college student who is reading about 5 years below his expected reading level. He needs challenging materials. Jonathan is extremely interested in travel. This article is a good selection for him. The excerpt below is the *last half* of the recording made for Jonathan.

>Jonathan: College sophomore; RL: 7.0; LCL: Superior
>Article: "Hong Kong: Get it While it's Hot" by Lauren Cobb
>RL of the Article: About 10.0
>Gap: 3 years
>How to Record:
>>PACE: Fairly slow, about 75 WPM
>>PHRASING: Short phrases, about 3-5 words per phrase
>>EXPRESSION: Slightly exaggerated
>>LENGTH: About 2 minutes

"Hong Kong: Get it While it's Hot"

Across the harbor is Hong Kong Island, a jumble of verdant mountains trimmed with white high-rises and encircled by jade green seas. Most visitors are drawn here by Hong Kong's flashy nightlife and reputation as a shopper's paradise. Yet beyond Hong Kong's preoccupation with commerce is something far more intriguing: a fragile, hybrid culture of Western capitalism built precariously on the edge of ancient Asia. Like a mirage shimmering in a modern city, one catches sudden, disturbing glimpses of another world, which over time asserts a strange fascination, as if Hong Kong sent out delicate clinging tendrils, sweet as opium and just as seductive.

Jonathan, we'll continue with the article about Hong Kong on the next tape side. Please rewind this tape. That ends this recording.

Sample Recordings For Groups and Individual Students

Courtesy, Hillcrest Elementary School, Lake Stevens School District, Everett, WA.

Chapter 6

Organizing the Teaching Materials and Grouping Students

Five Steps To Organizing the Books and Tapes

Most teachers tape record a few books to start, find that the method produces excellent results, and then decide to record a large number of books. Therefore, it's important to develop an organizational plan. The materials for the recorded book method should be organized so that youngsters can easily locate, use and return them.

First, books should be selected based on the quality of the writing, and the students' language-comprehension levels, reading levels, and interests. Next, the books and tapes should be coded so that they can be located easily by students. A decision will need to be made regarding how much to record on each tape cassette. After a small amount of text is recorded, the tape recording should be used with a group of students and, if necessary, re-recorded. Finally, the books and tape cassettes should be organized and stored. The five steps that follow can be used as a guide for organizing and storing the books and accompanying tape cassettes.

Courtesy, Robert W. Carbonaro School, District 24, Valley Stream, NY.

Step 1. Code the Books and Tape Cassettes

Many global teachers like to code books and their accompanying tapes in the manner described below.

A global coding strategy...

1. Number each page in the book consecutively. Be certain that the pages are numbered. If they are not, paginate them. The numbers will enable you to give the listener page cues as you record, and will help the student to keep his/her place in the story.

2. Code the tapes. Write or type the name of the book on a label. Make one label for each tape cassette. Then affix a label to the side of each tape cassette. Next, number each tape side consecutively.

Figure 6-A. A global strategy for coding the tape cassettes is to affix a label to the tape cassette that contains the title of the book and the pages recorded.

An analytic coding strategy...

Analytics generally are more concerned with efficiency than are globals. Many analytics prefer to number and color-code the books and tape cassettes, and then group all the tape cassettes together, all the books together, etc. This procedure enables more than one student to read the same book, provided there are multiple copies of the book. One way to code books and tape cassettes analytically is described below.

1. Number each page consecutively. This will enable the recorder to provide page cues for the reader.

2. Code the books. Number each book consecutively. Write the number of the book with an indelible marker on a sticker, and place it on the upper left-hand corner of the book cover.

3. Code the tapes. Use a fine-tipped, indelible marker to write the number of the book and the numbers of the tape sides on the spine of the cassette.

Figure 6-B. An analytic strategy for coding the tapes is to assign corresponding numbers to each book and tape. These numbers can then be used on record-keeping charts.

Step 2. Decide the Amount to be Recorded on Each Tape Side

Plan exactly how much will be recorded on each tape side. For example, if it is decided to record about three minutes on each tape side, and in that period of time four pages can be read, then the book should be divided into three- to five-page sections, depending upon the amount of print on each page and whether the section ends in a logical place. Write down the page numbers that will be recorded on each tape side. Record only side one. Then monitor and adjust the recording for that book, as described in step 3.

Step 3. Monitor and Adjust the Recordings

After recording only the first tape of one book, ask the students if they like the book, are able to follow the pace, and if there is sufficient time for them to turn pages, look at the pictures, and find the first line of print on each page. If most of them can read the pages fluently after two or three repetitions, then the length of the recording is probably just right.

Based on student recommendations, the pace, phrasing, expression and amount recorded can be adjusted. If necessary, the number of pages that will be recorded on each tape side should be recalculated. Step 3 will not be necessary before recording each book. After monitoring and adjusting a few times, the person recording should be able to tape record with the correct pace, phrasing , expression, and in the right amounts for that group of students.

To make the recordings permanent...

To make permanent tape recordings that cannot be erased, punch out the small rectangles on the spine of the tape cassette (see Figure 6-C).

Figure 6-C.

Step 4. Store the Materials

The books and tapes can be stored either globally or analytically. Examples of each strategy are described below.

A global storage strategy...

Many global teachers like to organize by topic. Since a book can be thought of as one topic, globals often store together everything related to one book. To store materials globally, place a book, the accompanying tape cassettes, and perhaps a small game about the book, in a plastic bag or envelope. Plastic bags with handles usually work quite well, and can be hung on hooks near a comfortable reading area.

Figure 6-D. A global strategy is to place all the materials related to one book together, in an envelope or plastic bag.

An analytic storage strategy...

As noted previously, analytics are generally more concerned with efficiency than are globals. By grouping the books together, the tape cassettes together, and the related materials together, more students can use the materials. For example, John may be reading *Charlotte's Web*. If *Charlotte's Web* is stored globally in a plastic bag, then John will have the plastic bag containing the materials near him, making it difficult for anyone else to use them until he has finished. But if there are multiple copies of the book, and the materials are stored separately, then John could conceivably be working with Tape Side 1 of *Charlotte's Web*, while a classmate is working with Tape Side 6.

Figure 6-E. An analytic storage strategy is to store separately each item that relates to one book. In this photo, for example, there are sequentially numbered books (1), coordinated tapes (2), coordinated writing activity cards (3), coordinated games (4), programmed audio cards that are coordinated with the books (5), and coordinated skill cards (6).

Step 5. Design Record-Keeping Charts

A record-keeping chart is very useful. It can serve as a guide for coding the tape cassettes and for tape recording them, *and* it can be used to keep a record of each student's progress. The chart can be duplicated and a copy can be placed in each student's folder.

In the chart reproduced below, notice that the books are listed down the left-hand column and a column is provided to indicate the date the book was begun and completed by the student. The pages to be recorded on each tape side are listed across the chart. For example, the first book on this chart, *The Monkeys and the Water Monster*, has pages 28 to 32 recorded on the fifth tape side; whereas, the third book on the list, *Pandas*, ends at tape side four, which has pages 24 to 29 recorded on it.

Book No.	Date(s)	Book title and author	TAPE SIDE AND PAGES									
			1	2	3	4	5	6	7	8	9	10
1		Monkeys & Water Monster by B. Chardier	7-11	12-15	16-23	24-27	28-32	33-38	39-43	44-48		
2		Bigger Giant by N. Green	3-9	10-17	18-23	24-30	24-29					
3		Pandas by R. L. Gross	2-8	9-17	18-23	24-29						

Figure 6-F. A chart placed in each student's folder makes record-keeping easy. This chart is reprinted from Teaching Students to Read Through Their Individual Learning Styles *by Marie Carbo, Rita Dunn and Kenneth Dunn, New Jersey: Prentice Hall, 1986.*

How to Color-Code the Books and Tape Cassettes

Color-coding helps children to find materials quickly, and to return them to their proper place. It can eliminate the need to help students locate and return materials.

To color code the books, place colored stickers on the books according to the level, subject, or whichever system you use to organize the resources. Then number those stickers depending upon whatever number was assigned to the book. The spines of the tape cassettes also can be color-coded so that each corresponds to the color of its companion book. Do this before writing the number of the book onto the cassette spine.

Book No.	Date(s)	Book title and author	TAPE SIDE AND PAGES									
			1	2	3	4	5	6	7	8	9	10
1		Monkeys & Water Monster by B. Chardier	7-11	12-15	16-23	24-27	28-32	33-38	39-43	44-48		

Figure 6-G.

How to Work With Individuals, Small Groups and Large Groups

There are many ways to organize groups. To a large extent, the size of the group will dictate the strategies that probably will work best. The smaller the group, the greater the possibility for individualizing the program; the larger the group, the more likely it is that students will need to work with the recordings in groups.

From the ideal to the acceptable...

The Ideal — A Totally Individualized Program. The ideal way to use the recorded book method is to make tape recordings for individual students. Individual recordings make it easy to select the books that will be of greatest interest to the student, and recordings can be made in exactly the right amounts, with the correct pace and phrasing. Making individual tape recordings for students, however, is the most time-consuming strategy, and is most likely to be used by teachers who are responsible for small groups of students, or teachers of large groups who use the procedure with just a few of their poorest readers. This technique of tape recording books for individual students provides differentiated instruction. *Students have made the greatest progress when they proceed at their own pace with personalized recordings.*

Almost Ideal — Students Progressing at Their Own Pace. The next best approach for the recorded book method is to find out which topics and books are of interest to a group. Record reading materials that reflect those interests, and allow the students to work at their own pace at individual tape players with headsets. Students can learn at their own pace with books that have been programmed and recorded for a group. For instance, these three youngsters are in the same group, but are moving at three very different rates:

Student learning at a rapid pace:
Day 1 - Book 1, Sides 1 and 2
Day 2 - Book 2, Sides 1 and 2
Day 3 - Book 2, Sides 3 and 4
Day 4 - Book 4, Sides 1 and 2
Day 5 - Book 4, Sides 3 and 4

Student learning at an average pace:
Day 1 - Book 1, Side 1
Day 2 - Book 1, Side 2 + supplementary word games
Day 3 - Book 2, Side 1
Day 4 - Book 2, Sides 2 and 3
Day 5 - Book 2, Side 4 and supplementary word games

Student learning at a very slow pace:
Day 1 - Book 1, Side 1
Day 2 - Supplementary Audio Cards and Word Games
Day 3 - Book 1, Side 2
Day 4 - Supplementary Audio Cards and Word Games
Day 5 - Book 1, Sides 1 and 2 are repeated

Courtesy, Hillcrest Elementary School, Lake Stevens School District, Everett, WA.

Acceptable — Students Working in Small to Large Groups. The least ideal technique–but still effective–is to have a group of students listen to a book tape at a listening center. Obviously, this strategy is the least ideal of the three because the students' individual interests are less likely to be accommodated, and all youngsters will probably have to proceed at a similar pace. This procedure, however, is often the most efficient for any teachers who work with large numbers of students at one time.

If there is a listening center in a classroom, then groups of children (usually up to twelve, depending upon the number of headsets available), can listen to a recording of a story while they follow along in their book. Many teachers have found this to be a successful approach with their reading groups in general and their slow readers in particular.

For poor readers, it is often beneficial to introduce a story, have a pre-reading discussion, and then read the beginning of the story aloud to the students, slowly, as they follow along in their books. Next, the youngsters can listen to a recording of that same section, or the next portion of the story, a few times at a listening center, while they follow along in their books. Last, the youngsters discuss the story and re-read portions aloud while in their reading group.

Some teachers have used a book tape with an entire class, while the students follow along in their books. This technique can be part of any regular reading lesson. While this is not an ideal procedure, it still can produce some good gains in reading. Possibly, this occurs because many students will listen more intently to a tape cassette than to a person reading aloud.

Courtesy, Juanita Elementary School, Lake Washington School District, Kirkland, WA.

Chapter 7

Using Recorded Books in the Subject Areas With Older Students

The remainder of this chapter, beginning with the next section, was written by Sharon Briggs and Ginny Sorrell who teach social studies and English as a 7th grade interdisciplinary team. Not only did Briggs' and Sorrell's students perform much better in class and on tests in social studies and English, many improved in their reading skills as well.

The system designed by Briggs and Sorrell is an effective way to use book recordings with older students. Chapter 7 describes in detail how to replicate the Briggs/Sorrell book recording system in any intermediate or secondary class.

Having met both Sharon Briggs and Ginny Sorrell, I was extremely impressed by their dedication, enthusiasm, follow through, and, most especially, the sensitivity and understanding they have for their students. For example, they decided to use Walkman-type recorders because they "did not want to single kids out and make them feel different by having to wear institutional-sized headphones and grouping them separately from the rest of the class." The recordings in this program were also made available to the students during class and to take home.

I concur with the strategies described by Briggs and Sorrell in this chapter, particularly the different procedures that they devised to record text versus recreational reading. As they stated, texts were recorded as "directed reading assignments" and "focused students on main content points," whereas novels were recorded "for pleasure, in one smooth flow." But, there are a few suggestions that I would like to add to those of Briggs' and Sorrell's.

First, to increase the reading ability of students reading below grade level, direct the youngsters to re-listen two to four times to a small portion of the beginning of a recorded text. If possible, the students should read back that small section aloud very soon after a repeated listening. That technique would speed up gains in word recognition and fluency. Second, I believe that many poor readers in secondary groups would make much greater strides in reading, if the recorded book method described in Chapter 3 were added to the program described by Briggs and Sorrell. For poor readers, then, a few stories or book chapters should be recorded in very short segments, at a slower-than-usual pace.

Using Recorded Books in the Subject Areas With Older Students

Is success possible for at-risk students? If you mean improved grades, no failures among students using tapes, no moans or groans at the mention of reading, raised hands volunteering to answer questions during class discussions, fewer discipline problems, keeping up with the class and homework being done, then the answer is a resounding "Yes!"

At-risk students do want to learn, will accept help, and will continue to try when they experience success. Our students who are using the tapes are most decidedly succeeding, and they are not being singled out and removed from class. The curriculum is not being watered down for them, and they are able to keep up with class demands. The cost is a one-time expenditure amounting to less than that of two computers. The yield? A permanent support system that can be shared among any number of students and teachers. The bottom line? Happier, more productive students and happier, less-frustrated teachers, administrators, and parents.

Courtesy, Lake Braddock Secondary School, Fairfax County, VA. Photographs by Robert Samuels, Springfield, VA.

This chapter was contributed by Sharon Briggs and Ginny Sorrell. Briggs and Sorrell are a 7th Grade Interdisciplinary Team for the Fairfax County Public Schools, Virginia. They conduct excellent presentations on their recorded book system. To contact them, write to: Sharon Briggs, 5924 Veranda Drive, Springfield, VA 22152, or Ginny Sorrell, 13704 Springstone Ct., Clifton, VA 22024. They can also be reached at (703) 455-4958.

Background

At Lake Braddock Secondary School in Fairfax County, we do not group students according to ability, other than to provide GT classes for the gifted. As the years go on, however, more and more students with deficient reading skills are creeping into our classrooms, and the difference between students' abilities in a single classroom is widening. More "second-wave" immigrants are impacting on the school system; these students not only have difficulty learning English, but many also exhibit deficiencies in their own language. In addition, there have been significant changes in the traditional 1950's family structure. Couple this with increasing economic pressures which necessitate more parents working and a more hurried pace of life simply to survive, and the result is less free time for parents to spend reading with their children. Instead, children spend the majority of their time at home watching television. Part of our decline in literacy is a direct result of these factors.

One day in October 1987 we sat down to analyze the kids who were failing tests, not doing homework, not completing reading assignments, not bringing supplies and books to class, and those who were discipline problems. We realized that the common denominator was that these students did not read on grade level. If we could only teach them to read more fluently, we thought, perhaps we could turn their failure syndrome around. It seemed hopeless, though: we were already overburdened with the task of covering curriculum requirements as outlined by the Fairfax Co. *Program of Studies.* How on earth could we find time in our schedule to teach reading on top of everything else? Not only that, but the majority of our students did read on grade level or above--how could we single out some students for reading groups without damaging their self-esteem? What would the rest of the class be doing in the meantime? These kids had already failed to learn to read fluently even though they had been in reading groups every year of their elementary experience; phonics approaches hadn't worked, nor had any of the other methods their elementary teachers had tried. What made us think we could do any better?

All of a sudden it dawned on us: kids spend most of their time with a Walkman plastered on their heads, listening to music with never a book in sight. Maybe, we thought, just maybe, we could bring their practiced ears together with the printed page. Common sense and observation suggested to us that our "at-risk" students were not dumb: they were certainly capable of learning the words to the top 50 hits. As we thought about the ubiquity of the Walkman, we began a new line of reasoning. If they could learn words to songs, could they not learn text by hearing it, too? Extending this reasoning, we felt that if they were provided with verbatim audio tapes of the reading material in our textbooks and novels, they could read along while listening to a good role model, and eventually their reading fluency would increase. No longer would they slam a book shut because it was too hard and the words were too long – now they would be provided with a non-threatening surrogate teacher at their beck and call. Thus, three separate goals might be achieved: (l) students would be provided with the means to improve their reading skills; (2) kids could keep up with the content of both history and English classes, participate actively in class discussions and make better grades; (3) because of new successes, their self-esteem would naturally improve, leading to increased motivation to succeed in both our classes and in other classes as well. In the end, perhaps school would no longer be "a drag." But we asked ourselves, what if the students simply listened to the tapes without reading along–wouldn't that defeat our purpose for the taping program? The answer we came up with was an unequivocal "No!" – since our overall goal was to help at-risk students succeed so that they would stay in school. At the very least, they would be able to keep up with the content and improve their grades. In other words, we were looking at a win-win situation.

At this point, we made a decision to forego the traditional listening center where several students plug into a single outlet and listen to a tape at the same time, for two reasons: we did not want to make kids feel different, by having them wear institutional-sized headphones, and by grouping them separately from the rest of the class; we also wanted to allow them the flexibility of deciding when and where to listen and read, as well as the freedom to rewind the tape and re-hear any passage they weren't sure about. By supplying small Walkman-type recorders, they could stop reading and listening when they wanted to or, if time ran out in class, take the tape home, slip it into their own recorders and resume where they left off.

Figure 7-A. The authors of chapter 7, Sharon Briggs and Ginny Sorrell, with some of their seventh-grade students. Courtesy, Lake Braddock Secondary School, Fairfax County, VA.

Research Supporting a Taping Program

We haven't found any research that has been done on providing taped books to a regular classroom of students, ranging from extremely bright, high-achievers to less-skilled and unmotivated, not to mention the increasing number of ESL students in each classroom. (We are presently compiling research from our own classroom and plan to continue this research with more students next year). What we *have* found is research on Special Ed. kids and the value of read-along tapes for them, especially Marie Carbo's work with a variety of special kids including LD, speech-impaired, ED, ER, and other severe learning handicaps. She has developed a specific method of taping short segments of reading material, and her research shows as much as 2 ½ years of reading growth over a period of one year. We have also found references to the value of read-along tapes, from reading authorities such as Jim Trelease, in his *Read-Aloud Handbook*.

What we have learned from such authorities as Dr. Helene Hodges, Director of Research and Information at ASCD, is that at-risk students have their own learning styles and reading styles, which differ from the general population. The traditional methods of teaching these students have not been successful – and will not be successful – because they do not incorporate auditory, visual, tactual, and kinesthetic approaches in the teaching of reading.

How We Set Up the Program

Since that morning a year and a half ago, we have put our energies into our taping program. With money we received from local grants (Impact II, *Washington Post,* Fairfax County Minority Achievement, PTA grants), we purchased blank cassettes, labels, checkout cards, a Telex One-By-One high-speed tape duplicator that allowed us to make one copy from a master in two minutes, and a number of commercially-produced books-on-tape.

Next, we organized volunteers who gradually taped the reading material we use in our classes: the history textbook, *One Flag, One Land* (almost 700 pages long); *Light in the Forest* (117 pages); *JohnnyTremain* (269 pages); *Shane* (119 pages); *Roll of Thunder, Hear My Cry* (210 pages); *Summer of My German Soldier*. We also taped some recreational reading books: *Bridge to Terabithia* (128 pages), *Escape from Skull Mountain* (Hardy Boys mystery - 169 pages), *Tex, Do Bananas Chew Gum?*. Others are in the process of being taped. There is a difference in the way these books have been taped: the history textbook was taped as a directed reading assignment with verbal instructions focusing students on main content points and walking them through SQ3R (Survey, Question, Read, Recite, Review), for each chapter, while the novels were taped as one reads for pleasure, with no interruption of the smooth flow of the story.

We wrote the publishers of the books explaining the needs of our students and the taping program we were developing. We asked for permission to record their book so that non-fluent readers could read the content and listen to a fluent reader at the same time.

Our program works as follows: students check out tapes to use during reading time in class and for take-home use as well. Tapes are labeled, identified, and have check-out cards. Original tape masters are never checked out but are used to make copies for check-out. A permanent library of 30 copies of each history chapter and 20 copies of each novel chapter is available for all teachers to use. Classroom student librarians handle the check-in/check-out process with pride and enthusiasm.

We have found that even good readers don't read, so in addition to supporting our own classroom content programs with teacher-generated tapes, we have purchased a number of commercially-produced books on tape for recreational reading. This includes a number of cliffhangers (usually the first one-third of the book). The idea here is to encourage all students to read more and to provide opportunities for all students to enjoy the audio as well as visual stimulation. As one of our students said recently, "It's cool to be listening to a Walkman in class!"

Results To Date

We started small the first year because we did not know what to expect: we chose to concentrate on eight of our least able students. We were not able to begin supplying these students with tapes until our first grant (a *Washington Post* mini-grant) was funded in January 1988. Until this time, most of these students opted out of classroom discussions and appeared disinterested, and some were discipline problems who needed constant attention. Gradually they seemed to sit up and pay closer attention. Several began tentatively to join in class discussions. They didn't seem quite so belligerent. And wonder of wonders, most of the time they now even knew what page we were on when we called on them to answer questions. In other words, these kids began to succeed, at least in our subjective evaluations. We were elated. We felt we had hit upon something which was worth a more concentrated effort. Therefore, when the 1988/9 school year rolled around we were ready to collect somewhat more scientific data.

During 1988/9, twenty-six of the 31 deficient readers within our class load of 117 opted to check out tapes. Since we had no reading scores at the beginning of the year for our incoming seventh graders, we asked students to identify themselves if they had reading problems (comprehension, speed, fluency): 16 identified themselves. After we received the DRP (Degrees of Reading Power), scores from the elementary feeder schools in late October, we added another 14 students to the list based on the fact that they scored 10 or more DRP points below the level needed to read the history textbook comfortably. Later a new ESL student transferred in and identified himself as needing tapes to help him understand the reading. We subsequently tested all 31 students using the Gates-MacGinitie reading assessment to give us additonal data, especially reading comprehension information.

PILOT RESULTS – PERSONAL GROWTH AND ACADEMIC ACHIEVEMENT: Teachers observed that participants became more active and informed in classroom discussions and assumed more classroom leadership roles.

The 26 at-risk students in the program earned a 2.6 (C+) overall average in history and a 2.2 (C) in English, based on the traditonal 4.0 scale; the five students who did not participate earned an average 1.2 (D) in history and 0.8 (D-) in English. These grades were earned objectively and according to the same criteria used for the other students in the heterogeneous classes. No adaptations other than the tapes were made for the at-risk students; they were required to turn in the same homework assignments, adhere to the same deadlines, participate in class discussions, and take the same tests as the rest of the students. The content was not watered down, and the students were not involved in pull-out programs.

PILOT RESULTS – READING ACHIEVEMENT: In the seven months between a pre- and posttest in reading comprehension as measured by the Gates-MacGinitie Reading Test, the participating students gained an average of 1.2 years. Fifteen students had gains greater than 7 months, which could be expected as natural growth during that period. Since at-risk students generally despise reading and avoid it at all costs, they typically do not make normal gains during the school year. Thus the gain of 1.2 years probably represents a significantly greater gain for this population of students than it would for students without reading problems. Seven at-risk students made gains of 2.5 years or more, and one showed a gain of 4.1 years.

Other data suggest that these students began reading more frequently on a voluntary basis. For example, during a Reading Incentive Program hosted by the school's Media Center, a greater percentage of the 26 students in the read-along tapes program (85%) opted to participate than the intermediate school student body as a whole. Eighteen of these at-risk students (69%) read the six books in eight weeks required to "win" entrance to the movie/party which was the culminating activity of the incentive program. Altogether the at-risk students read 134 books.

How Can You Establish a Read-Along Taping Program?

We can't stress enough that you need to establish a permanent library of tapes to prevent wear-and-tear on your equipment and on yourself. It costs much less than purchasing supplementary textbooks or hiring another aide. It's also impossible for classroom teachers to tape, erase, and redub on a daily basis to meet the needs of the at-risk student, not to mention that the smaller duplicating machines will not withstand high volume usage. **NOTE:** setting up a permanent library allows tapes to be centrally located, shared and easily accessed by all teachers on a grade level or within the same subject area. Thus, the expenditures below reflect a one-time expense not per teacher but per grade level. These expenses would not recur from year to year other than to replace lost or broken tapes or to add to the collection or library. As teachers are rarely on the same chapter of their textbooks with their colleagues at the same time, or are rarely using the same novels at the same time, sharing is natural. Obviously, if you have a media services facility in your locality, the easiest route would be to let them do your tape duplicating and make the labels for your tapes. If not, the following can be used as a guideline.

Elementary Classroom Situation

Assumption: 5-6 students (approximately the lowest 20% of a class of 30)

Material Requirements:
- Tape duplicating machine which duplicates one copy at a time per master (approx. $375)
- Good quality tape recorder-- this is essential because your masters must be clear and free from background noise (some loss of quality will inevitably occur in duplicating copies from a master) (approx. $400)
- Tape eraser (magnetic bulk eraser = $25.00)
- Blank cassettes: approx. 25 cassettes per novel (35-45 pages can be taped on one 60-min cassette, so one novel averages 4 cassettes; a permanent library should be established which contains 6 copies of each master, servicing 6 students at a time). Cost: approx. $0.65 per cassette.
- 5-6 Walkman playback-only tape players (approx. $25.00 each) for students to use during class while reading their book (not to be checked out overnight)
- batteries for Walkmans (4 AA's per Walkman)
- Check-out cards and envelopes for each cassette
- 4 labels per cassette: one for check-out card, one on envelope, one on cassette, and one on spine of cassette box (it's easiest to type continuous roll of labels, i.e., those designed for computers)

Human Requirements:
- Recorder(s): fluent readers (teacher, administrator, parent, National Honor Society student-- try for male and female readers); NOTE: not all volunteers read well on tape, some informal screening will be necessary on your part.
- Typist(s): to type labels
- Organizer who can spend significant time coordinating the recording, labeling storage, and distribution of tapes (could be reading resource teacher, aide, parent volunteer, other resource teacher)

Secondary Classroom Situation

Assumption: 24-30 at-risk students per teacher (defined as lowest 20% of normal class load 120-150 students)

Equipment:
- Tape duplicating machine which duplicates three copies at a time from a master and also erases as it dubs (approx. $1500)
- Blank cassettes: approx. 1000 (this will allow for a permanent library of 30 copies of masters; for example, one 60-min. master per chapter of content material in a textbook; or 30 copies of 7 novels averaging 5 masters per novel)

Remainder of equipment and human resources is same as that for elementary classroom situation.

How To Record Read-Along Tapes

First, ask yourself what your objective is for the lesson. Are you dealing with a novel or a textbook? Are the students reading for pleasure or for knowledge? This will determine the approach you should take for the recording.

Second, round up the very best quality tape recorder you can find. Remember, you are dubbing masters from which many copies will be made. These masters will form the basis of your tape library for years. What you don't want to do is redub them because their quality is poor. (We speak from experience!)

Tips for All Recording:
1. Set the volume control on your recorder to minimum – this will prevent distortion. The listener will still be able to increase the volume to a level which is comfortable.
2. Find a space to record which will have minimum background noise and decent acoustics. A bathroom, although not the most comfortable place in which to record, will probably produce the clearest tapes short of a professional studio.
3. Keep your mouth within six inches of the microphone.
4. Allow about ten seconds of blank tape before you begin recording, so that the beginning of your recording will not be cut off when you duplicate it.
5. State the chapter number, title of the chapter, and page number before you begin the actual narration.
6. Try to end each side of a tape at a natural stopping place such as the end of a chapter or a break on a page.
7. Immediately after you record, label your original tape with the pages or chapter(s) contained on it, write the word "ORIGINAL" prominently on the tape and store it separately from the copies you subsequently make. Never check out your originals!

Tips for Recording Novels:
1. If there is dialect in the novel, practice reading it before you record.
2. Read at normal speed, the same speed with which you would read orally to your class. The purpose is to help these students learn to read fluently by giving them a fluent role model, not to enunciate every word individually so that the student focuses on a single word. Many of their problems stem from the fact that they linger on a word until they get it exactly right, rather than plowing ahead and getting the sense of the sentence through context.
3. Read with inflection and feeling.
4. If you realize that you've made a mistake, go back and redub that section, especially if the inflection you put on a word might cause confusion as far as meaning is concerned. A small quantity of minor errors need not be corrected -- it won't do any harm if the students realize that even fluent readers make mistakes from time to time.

5. Try to end each side of the tape at a natural break–having the tape run out in the middle of a line is disconcerting, and causes havoc in labeling the tapes.
6. Students listening to the tapes should complete the exact same assignments you assign to the rest of the class: journal writing, discussion questions, projects book talks, etc.

Tips for Recording Textbooks:
1. Familiarize yourself with what is in the chapter before you begin recording.
2. Use SQ3R. Before you begin reading the text, focus the student's attention on any vocabulary or key facts which might be highlighted at the beginning of the chapter. Next, ask the student to turn to the end of the chapter, and read along with you the questions at the end. Explain that he should look for answers to each of these questions as he reads along with you.
3. Read the text verbatim without interjecting any explanation of the content. The only time you should interrupt the exact wording of the text is at the beginning of the recording, at the end, and any time questions may appear (for example, if a chapter is broken into sections). Then use a simple statement such as, "See if you can answer the following questions:..."
4. When you have finished reading the chapter, again focus the student on the questions or key facts at the end of the chapter.
5. Students using tapes should answer the same questions and do the same assignments you assign to the rest of the class. They should be expected to participate in class discussions to the same extent as the rest of the class.

Materials To Help At-Risk Students

Complete Books on Tape:
Are You There God? It's Me, Margaret (commercial production)
Bridge to Terabithia :The Chocolate War (commercial)

Materials To Help At-Risk Students

Complete Books on Tape:
Are You There God? It's Me, Margaret (commercial production)
Bridge to Terabithia :The Chocolate War (commercial)
Do Bananas Chew Gum?
From the Mixed-Up Files of Mrs. Basil E. Frankweiler (commercial)
Johnny Tremain
Light in the Forest
No Promises in the Wind
The Not-Just-Anybody Family (commercial)
The Pinballs (commercial)
The Pistachio Prescription (commercial)
Roll of Thunder, Hear My Cry
The Secret of Skull Mountain (Hardy Boys volume)
Shane
Summer of My German Soldier
Thirteen Ways to Sink a Sub (commercial)
Tuck Everlasting (commercial)

Cliffhangers(all of the following are commercially-produced):
Anastasia At Your Service
Blubber
Can You Sue Your Parents for Malpractice?
The Cat Ate My Gymsuit
A Day No Pigs Would Die
Divorce Express
Down a Dark Hall
House with a Clock in Its Walls
Interstellar Pig
Killing Mr. Griffin
Nothing's Fair in Fifth Grade
The Phantom Tollbooth
Snowbound
Stranger with My Face
There's a Bat in Bunk Five
Where the Red Fern Grows

Available in the Library:
The Cat Ate My Gymsuit
A Day No Pigs Would Die
Divorce Express
Down a Dark Hall
Dr. Jekyll and Mr. Hyde

Fantastic Tales of Ray Bradbury
Huckleberry Finn
The Merry Adventures of Robin Hood
The Pistachio Prescription
Shel Silverstein
Snowbound
The Time Machine
Treasure Island
Where the Red Fern Grows

Kits:

Comprehension Skills (accompanied by tapes)
Reading in the Content Area (accompanied by tapes)
Single Skills (no tapes)
Aids for History:
One Flag One Land - taped completely; each chapter on separate tape
Kit: *The Basic Illustrated History of America* (comic book format)

Appendix A

Designing Resources to Supplement the Book Recordings

Which Students Need These Materials?
Some youngsters have reading styles that match the recorded book method. They make rapid progress in reading using only the tape recorded book program described in Chapter 3. Others, however, need reinforcement of the words presented on the tape recording. It may be difficult for them to learn due to a low language proficiency, memory problems, and/or perceptual deficits.

How the Supplementary Resources Help Poor Readers
Many poor readers are global, tactile and kinesthetic. They learn well from "hands-on," global resources. For optimum reading progress, it is absolutely essential that global youngsters practice their reading skills using exercises drawn directly from the story context. Here is a procedure that is especially helpful for global students:

1. *Step 1.* First the story should be read, and discussed so that global youngsters will understand the context of the lessons that will follow.
2. *Step 2.* Next, the students can practice cartain skills with exercises drawn from the characters, vocabulary and events of the story. Preferably, these should be in a game-like format. It is advisable to design supplementary resources that give practice in the vocabulary presented on the recording, while involving the students' tactile and kinesthetic modalities.

Steps 1 and 2 will ensure that most primary youngsters and poor readers are learning through what is usually their cognitive style (global), and their perceptual strengths (tactile/kinesthetic, and sometimes, visual).

Three Types of Supplementary Materials
Three global resources that have been very successful are: audio cards, tactile/kinesthetic materials, and writing activity cards. A few samples of each resource is provided in this appendix. Additional samples can be found in *Teaching Students to Read Through Their Individual Learning Styles* (Carbo, Dunn and Dunn).

Figure A-1. These audio cards are the beginning of a set of cards for the book, The Story About Ping. *Ideally, the phrases from the book retell the story. The last few cards can provide practice of words in isolation. These cards have been numbered in sequential order in the upper right-hand corner. The number of the book and the tape side appear in the lower left-hand corner of the card.* The Story About Ping *is book #6 in this series. The phrases have been taken from the first tape side of the book..*

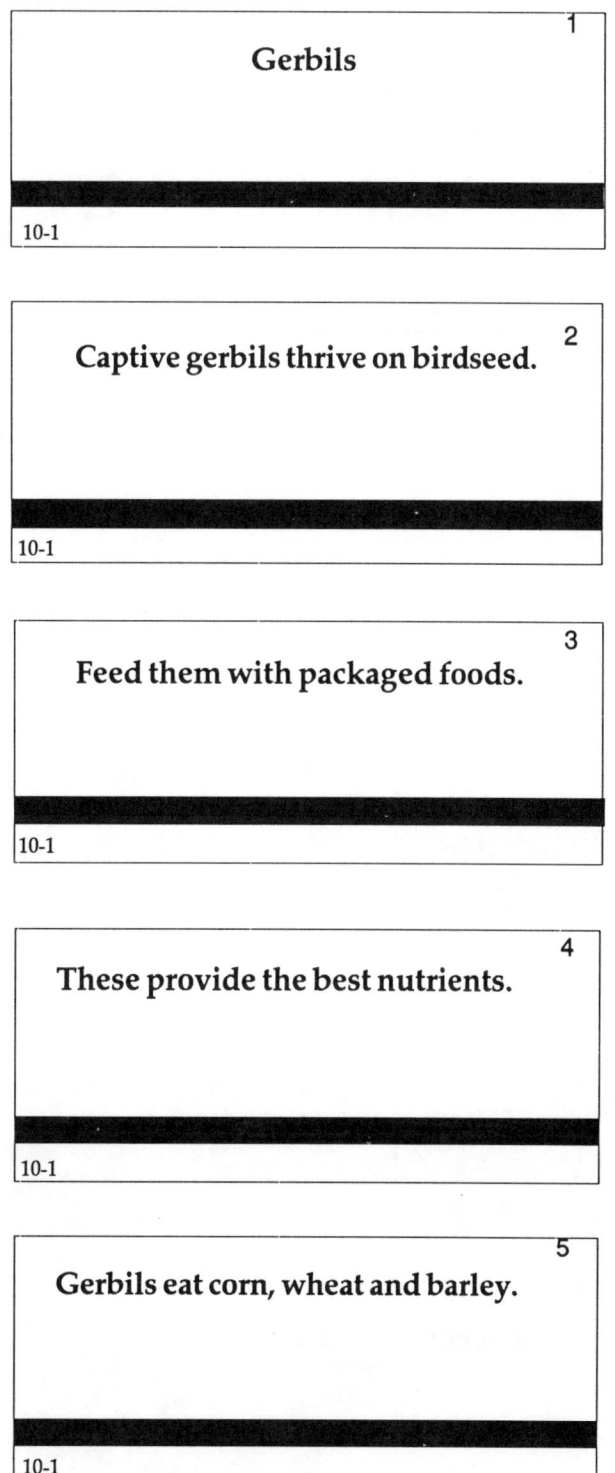

Figure A-2. For more difficult books, place phrases from the story on cards. Words from these phrases can be practiced in isolation, after they have been practiced in phrases.

Figure A-3. Task cards are ideal for matching activities such as: sequencing events, developing sight vocabulary, synonyms, etc. If the cards are cut in distinctive shapes, as shown, they become self-checking. If no distinct shapes are made, then the student can self-check on the back of the cards.

**Book: *Sport Cards*
Skill: Vocabulary Development**

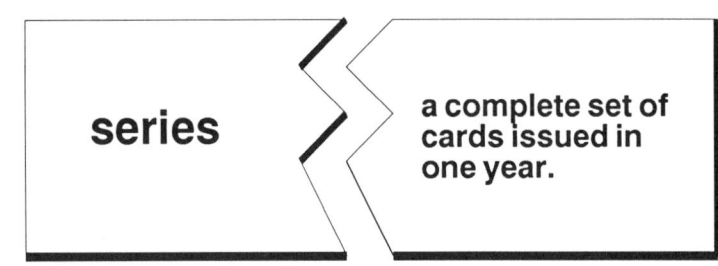

Bingo

Book: *The Martian Chronicles*
Skill: Vocabulary Development

ecology	dispose	debris	mock
biologist	ancient	scheme	taunt
adviser	menace	audience	orbit
squint	precise	hoax	alien

Figure A-4. The game format provides repetition in a format that most children enjoy. Both bingo and dominoes can be used for any matching exercise, such as matching synonyms, antonyms, words and their definitions, etc.

**Book: *Charlotte's Web*
Skill: Sequencing Events**

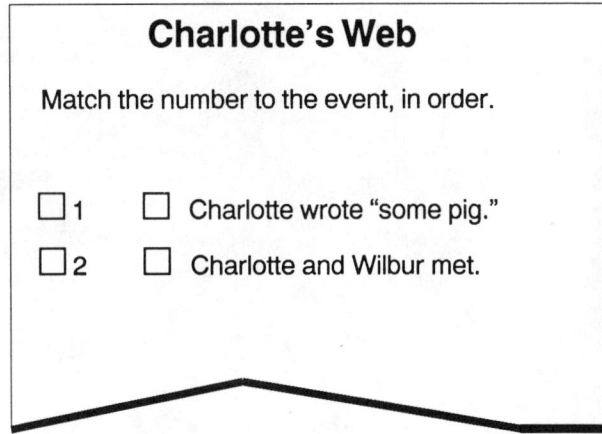

Figure A-5. Electroboards are super-high-interest. When the buzzer sounds and/or the light goes on, you can see a student's face brighten. These devices can be used for most matching activities. Specific directions for constructing electro-boards and pik-a-holes (Figure A-6), are in *Teaching Students to Read Through Their Individual Learning Styles* (Carbo, Dunn and Dunn).

Figure A-6. Pik-a-hole is a good device for any exercises involving multiple choice. The student places an object like a pencil in the correct opening. Only the card with the correct answer is constructed so that it can be removed while the pencil is in the correct opening.

**Book: *Charlotte's Web*
Skill: Drawing Conclusions**

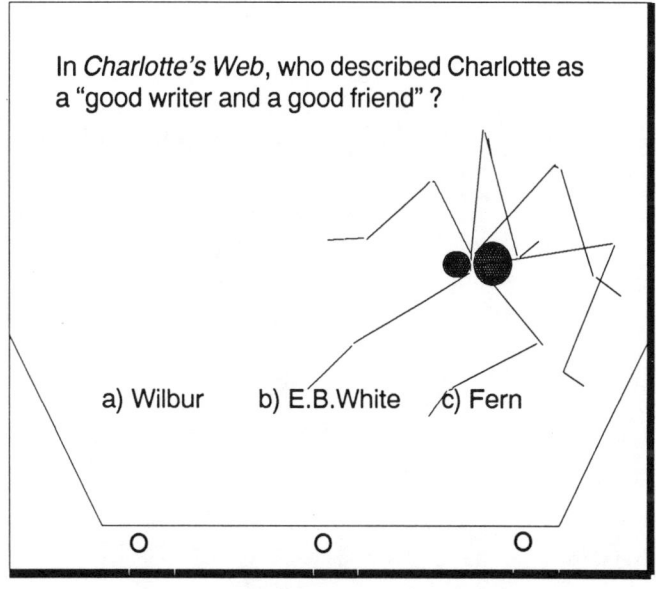

Courtesy, Sacred Heart Seminary, Hempstead, NY.

**Book: *Tom Sawyer*
Skill: Character Analysis**

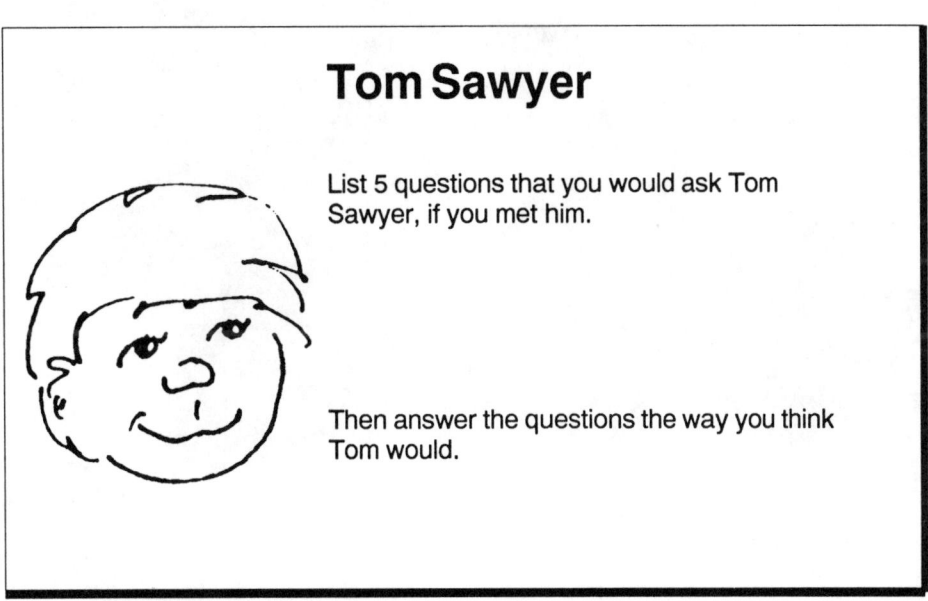

**Book: *Let's Be Enemies*
Skill: Identifying With Characters in a Story
　　　　Developing Self-Understanding**

Figure A-7. One way to stimulate children's writing is to place a drawing from a book on an index card, plus a writing activity related to the story.

Courtesy, Glynn County Schools, Brunswick, GA.

Appendix B

Schedules and Record-Keeping Charts

All the forms depicted in this appendix may be photocopied for classroom use.

Courtesy, Robert W. Carbonaro School, District 24, Valley Stream, NY.

Figure B-1. The form to the right is used to keep a record of which book tapes the student has completed. Note that books are listed down the left-hand side in numerical order. Columns 1-10 contain the pages recorded on each tape side. When a student completes a tape side satisfactorily, he/she can color in the corresponding tape side box with a yellow marker. The column headed, "Date," can contain the date the book was begun, the date it was completed, or both. A blank version of this form is on page 93.

BOOK TAPES

DATES	NO.	BOOK TITLE	BOOK TAPE SIDE AND PAGES										
			1	2	3	4	5	6	7	8	9	10
	1	Monsters of the Sea	3-6	7-11	12-17	18-21	22-27	28-33	34-38	39-42	43-48	
	2	All Pro Basketball	2-7	9-13	14-17	18-22	23-29	30-34				
	3	Reggie Jackson	1-3	3-6	7-10	10-12	13-16	17-21	94-97	98-101	102-104	104-106
	4	Charms & Spells, Witches & Demons	1-4	4-7	7-10	10-12	13-15	16-18	24-25	26-27	27-29	29-32
			32-34	35-36	36-38	38-41	41-44	45-47	47-49	49-51	51-53	53-55
	5	Dr. Jekyll & Mr. Hyde	78-80	84-85	85-86	86-87						
	6	Sinbad's Seven Voyages	4-6	6-10	10-12	13-15	31-33	33-36	36-38	38-41		
	7	Adventures of Tom Sawyer	18-20	20-23	23-25	25-28						
	8	Frankenstein	11-14	14-17	17-20	20-23	24-26	26-28	28-30	31-34		

Figure B-2. This is a blank version of Figure B-1. After deciding which books will be recorded, and which pages will be recorded on each tape side, this form can be completed and stapled into a youngster's folder.

BOOK TAPES

DATES	NO.	BOOK TITLE	BOOK TAPE SIDE AND PAGES									
			1	2	3	4	5	6	7	8	9	10

Figure B-3. The form to the right is used to keep a record of how a student reads aloud after listening to a book recording. It includes the date of the reading, the title of the book and tape side, the teacher's comments about the student's reading, and any words with which the youngster has had difficulty. Both this form and the one pictured in Figure B-2, may be photocopied and stapled into a folder for each student.

Name _____

Individualized Reading

DATE	BOOK	TAPE SIDE	COMMENTS	WORDS TO STUDY

Schedules and Record-Keeping Charts

Figure B-4. The form to the right is a weekly schedule for one student. On it, the teacher would indicate the number of the book and tape side completed by the youngster. An efficient procedure would be to color-code and number the tape cassettes and books. Then, on a schedule such as this, the teacher need only write: "Yellow 6(4)," which would mean the fourth tape side of the sixth book in the yellow series of books. If the supplementary materials (audio cards, games, etc.), are also color-coded and numbered, then the teacher need only write the color and item number in the appropriate box.

Depending upon the maturity of the students, some can design their own programs or use a form such as this one to note the work that they have already completed.

Name _____ Date _____

	Book Tape	Audio Cards	Skill Cards	Writing Activity	Games
Monday					
Tuesday					
Wednesday					
Thursday					
Friday					

Appendix C

Charts For Identifying Students' Favorite Books

Courtesy, Glynn County Schools, Brunswick, GA.

Charts for Identifying Students' Favorite Books

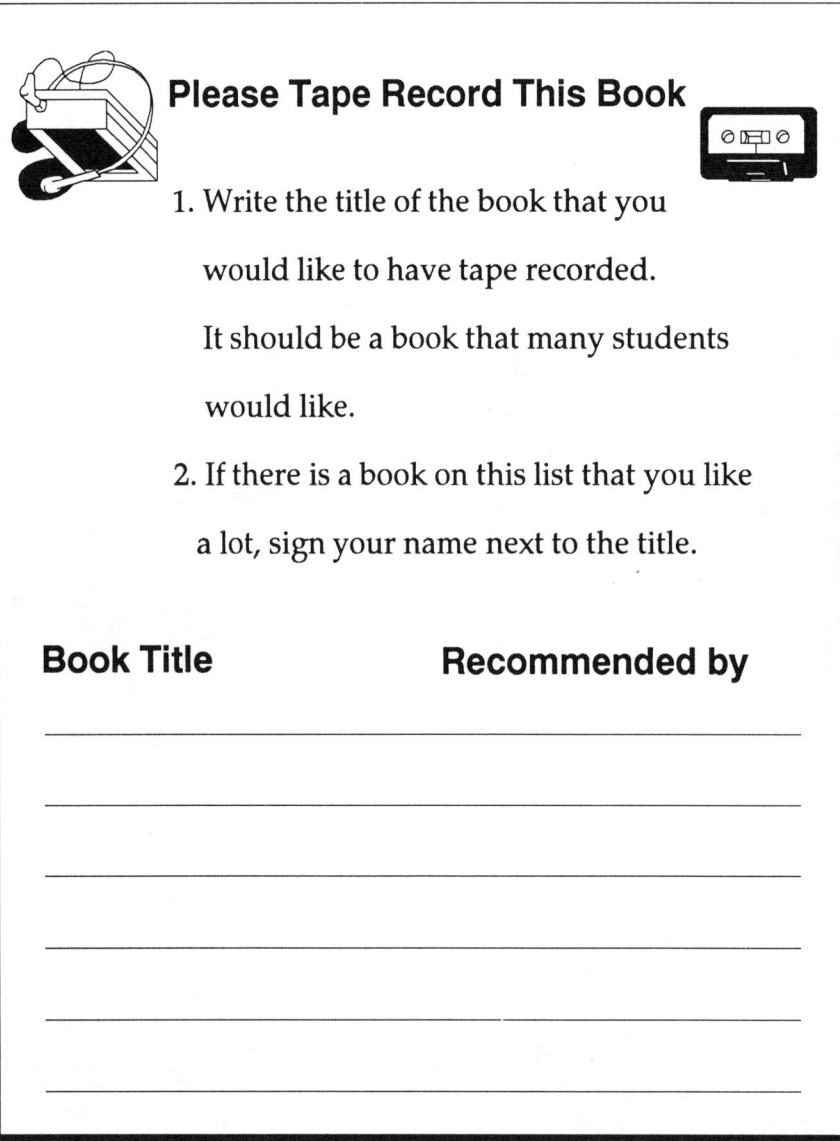

Figure C-1. A larger version of this chart can help the teacher to accumulate a library of recorded books that are of great interest to a group of students. On this chart, the students can write down the titles of books they would like recorded, and sign their name next to books that have been recommended by other students. In this way, the number of students who are interested in a particular title becomes apparent.

Charts for Identifying Students' Favorite Books

Mystery Book Club

Read 5 mystery books to become a member!

Add your name to the list.

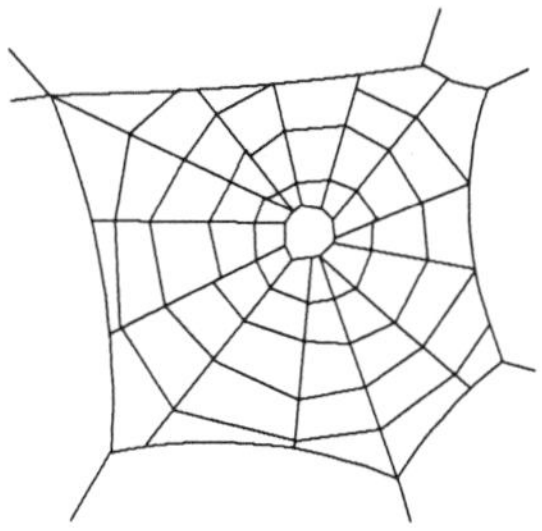

Date	Name	Favorite Mystery Book

Figure C-2. A large or small replica of this chart can be made for any type of book club, such as: "Science Book Club," or "Jokes and Riddles Book Club." Time can be set aside during the school day for students to meet in their book clubs. The purpose of the chart and meetings would be to stimulate the students to read independently and to discuss their favorite books with peers.

Charts for Identifying Students' Favorite Books

Book Winners

Our class voted on the 10 best books

we read this month.

These are the books that won.

_____

_____

_____

_____

_____

_____

Figure C-3. A large chart of this figure can be made. Students then nominate and vote on their favorite books. The books can be listed on the chart and the results posted.

Appendix D

Recommended Books For Tape Recording

List 1 - Books Recorded by Marie Carbo for Poor Readers (Gr. 1-6)
List 2 - Books Recorded by Marie Carbo for Poor Readers (Gr. 4-14)
List 3 - Predictable Books for Young, Beginning Readers (K-3)
List 4 - Low-Level Big Books (K-2)
List 5 - High-Interest, Low-Readability Books (Gr. 4-10)
List 6 - High-Interest Books for Children (K-6)
List 7 - Excellent Read-Aloud Books (K-8)
List 8 - Books for All Grades, Many Award Winners (K-12)
List 9 - Books Older Kids Love (Gr. 5-12)

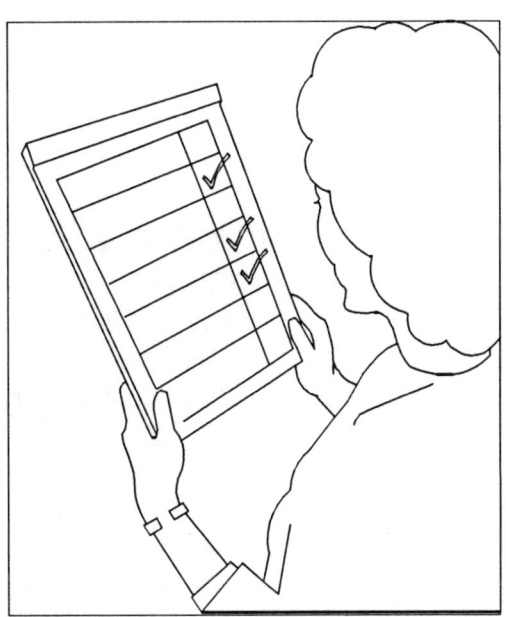

List 1
(Poor Readers, Grades 1-6)
(Average/Good Readers, Grades 1-4)

This list contains some of the books tape recorded by Marie Carbo for severely learning disabled students. The books are sequenced in order of difficulty, and were selected so that the reading level of each book is gradually increased in small increments. Many of these books are available from: Scholastic, Inc. P.O. Box 7501, 2931 E. McCarty St., Jefferson City, MO 65102.

RL:Gr. 1

The Happy Egg
The Carrot Seed
Cat and Dog
Go Away, Dog
Did You Ever See?
I Was Walking Down the Road
A Bug In a Jug
One, Two, Three, Going to Sea
A Kiss For Little Bear
Green Eggs and Ham
Look Out, Mrs. Doodlepunk!
My Box and String
Indian Two Feet and His Horse
In My Backyard
The Magic Fish
Let's Be Enemies
The Littlest Rabbit
Silly Sam
The Very Hungry Caterpillar

RL:GR.1-2

The Mouse Book
A Tiny Family
The Gingerbread Man
Fortunately
Goodnight, Richard Rabbit
The Country Cat
Nobody Listens to Andrew
Mr. Pine's Mixed-Up Signs
Mouse Tales
The Secret Kitten
Just in Time For the King's Birthday
I Can Keep a Secret
Henny Penny

Clifford's Tricks
Morris the Moose Goes to School
The Witch Next Door

RL:GR. 2-3

Rabbit & Skunk & Spooks
Crazy Zoo
The Little King, the Little Queen & the Little Monster
The Boy Who Would Not Say His Name
Rabbit & Skunk & the Big Fight
Not This Bear!
No Roses For Harry
Red Fox & His Canoe
Some Things Are Scary
One Fish, Two Fish, Red Fish, Blue Fish
Little Chestnut Tree Story
Too Many Rabbits
A Very Special House
Little Racoon & the Outside World
Cat In the Hat Comes Back

RL:GR. 3-4

Georgie
That's What Friends Are For
Olaf Reads
Case of the Hungry Stranger
The Man Who Didn't Wash His Dishes
The Magic Tablecloth, the Magic Goat and the Hitting Stick
Monkey Trouble
A Crocodile's Tale
Bread & Jam for Frances
The Story About Ping
Georgie & the Robbers
Ickle Bickle Robin

The Five Chinese Brothers
The Hungry Thing
Tumble
Sad Day, Glad Day
All Kinds of Babies

RL:GR.4-5
Monkeys & Water Monster
Bigger Giant
Pandas
How Animals Sleep
Adventures of Tom Thumb
The Great Whales

He's Your Dog, Charlie Brown
How to Care For Your Dog
Hidden Animals
What is That Alligator Saying?
Casey, the Utterly Impossible Horse
Harlem Globetrotters
Lonesome Bear
Encyclopedia Brown
Secrets of the Animal World
Henry Huggins
Paul Bunyan Swings His Axe
Ghost Stories
Charlotte's Web

List 2
(Poor Readers, Grades 5-10)
(Average/Good Readers, Grades 4-8)

This is a listing of some of the books recorded by Marie Carbo for twice-retained, seventh graders who were reading from 2 to 5 years below grade level. Many of the books are available from Scholastic (See List 1 for address). Another series of books that would be very good for this group of students is List 5, from Fearon.

RL:GR. 2-3
How Animals Sleep
Pandas
Frederick Douglas
Helen Keller
Monsters of the Sea
Wild Mammoth Hunters
Five True Horse Stories
Thomas Edison
He's Your Dog, Charlie Brown

RL:GR. 3-4
Facts-ination
Humans of Ziax II
Star Wars
Wonders of the Human Body
Spooky Stories
Birth of an Island
Deadly Creatures of the Sea
Master of Magic
Battlestar Gallactica
America's Favorite Sports Stars

RL:GR. 5-6
Sports Cards
Favorite Wild Animals
Charlotte's Web
All Pro Basketball
For the Love of Benjie
Reggie Jackson: Yankee Superstar
Science In Sports
Charms and Spells
Little Vic

RL:GR. 6-12
Martian Chronicles
Dr. Jekyll and Mr. Hyde
Sinbad's Seven Voyages
Adventures of Tom Sawyer
A Tree Grows in Brooklyn
Frankenstein
20 Grand Short Stories
Heroes of Greek Myth

RL:GR. 7-12
Blue Beard
Charles
The Monkey's Paw
The 1,000,000 Pound Bank Note
Man Who Wrote His Obituary
A Sick Call
Rocking Horse Winner
Poetry of Langston Hughes
Harrison Bergeron

List 3
(Poor Readers, Grades K-3)
(Average/Good Readers, Grades K-l)

All of the books on this list of predictable books for young, beginning readers have one or more of the following characteristics: "limited text per page, repeated pattern, refrain, rhyme, strong rhythm, and/or supportive illustrations" (Heald-Taylor, 1987). The complete list was reported by Gail Heald-Taylor in her excellent article, "Predictable Literature Selections and Activities for Language Arts Instruction," *The Reading Teacher*, October 1987, pp. 6-12.

Pattern Book Selections

***Most Predictable
Althea Can You Moo? London, England: Dinosaur Press, 1981.
What's for Lunch?, Eric Carle, New York, NY: Putnam, 1982.
Guinea Pig ABC, Kate Duke, New York, NY: E.P. Dutton, 1983.
Guinea Pigs Far and Near, Kate Duke, New York, NY: E.P. Dutton, 1984.
Trucks, Gail Gibbons, New York, NY: Thomas Y. Crowell, 1981.
Kittens from One to Ten, Mirra Ginsburg, New York, NY: Crown, 1980.
Bunny Sees, Hargrave Hands, London, England: Walker Books, 1985.
Where's Spot?, Eric Hill, New York, NY: Putnam, 1980.
I Can, Can You?, Petty Parish, New York, NY: Greenwillow, 1980.

**Very Predictable
My Name Is Alice, Jane Bayer, New York, NY: E.P. Hutton, 1984.
Across the Stream, Mirra Ginsburg, New York, NY: Puffin Books, 1985.
Seven Eggs, Meredith Hooper, London England: Patrick Hardy Books, 1985.
Home Sweet Home, Maureen Roffey, London, England: The Bodley Head, 1983.
Look, There's My Hat, Maureen Roffey, London, England, The Bodley Head, 1984.

*Predictable Selections
The Rose in My Garden, Arnold Lobel, New York, NY: Greenwillow, 1984.
Just Grandma and Me, Mercer Mayer, Racine, WI: Golden Books, 1983.
Quick as a Cricket, Audrey Wood, Purton, England: Child's Play (International), 1982.
The Napping House, Audrey Wood, New York, NY: Harcourt Brace Jovanovich, 1984.

List 4
(Poor Readers, Grades K-2)
(Average/Good Readers, Grades K-l)

These Big Books from Nellie Edge are a delight. They are excellent for recording. Not only are the books filled with wonderful rhymes and predictable, repeated language, but there are black-line masters for "fold-a-books," making it possible to provide copies of each book, very inexpensively, for every child in a class. In addition, Nellie Edge has books filled with finger plays and action rhymes, blank big books, teaching guides, cookbooks, and excellent high-frequency "word stamp sets." All are available from Resources for Creative Teaching, P. 0. Box 12399, Salem, OR 97309-0399.

Some of the delightful books from Nellie Edge are:

Make Friends With Mother Goose
Songs and Rhymes for a Rainy Day
Opposite Song
The Wheels on the Bus
Sing a Rainbow
Peanut Butter and Jelly
Goodnight Irene
I've Got a Cat
I've Got a Bunny
I've Got a Frog
I Can Read Colors
Jack-O-Faces
Teddy Bear, Teddy Bear
Down by the Bay
Mary Wore Her Red Dress
Over in the Meadow
Five Little Speckled Frogs

List 5
(Poor Readers, Grades 6-12)

These thin, paperback books are ideal for tape recording. The books are short, well written, and on topics of particular interest to students in the upper grades. Reading levels range from 4.5 to 6.4 while the interest level ranges from grades 6-1). They are available from Fearon, 500 Harbor Blvd., Belmont, CA 94022. Also available from Fearon are history, biography and classic books that are appropriate for high school students and adults

Fastback Crime and Detection Series
Beginner's Luck
The Blind Alley
Dressed Up for Murder
The Wet Good-bye

Fastback Mystery Series
Bill Waite's Will
Game for Fools
The Intruder
Mad Enough to Kill

Fastback Science Fiction Series
The Champion
Eden's Daughters
Just in Case
Vital Force

Fastback Sports Series
The Comeback
The Kid With the Left Hood
Marathon
The Rookie
The Sure Thing

Fastback Horror Series
The Disappearing Man
Mad Dog
Message for Murder
Now Power on Earth

Fastback Spy Series
The Cobra
Death in Any Language
The Last Hand
The Trap

Fastback Romance Series
Part of the Dream
For Always
Fifteen
Nobody knows But Me

List 6
(Poor Readers, Grades K-4)
(Average/Good Readers, Grades K-4)

The Wright Group was the first U.S. publisher to bring whole language books to the United States from Australia and New Zealand. This small listing of their large collection of excellent books is available from the Wright Group, 10949 Technology Place, San Diego, CA 92127.

Read-Together Big Books
Hairy Bear
Meanies
Mrs. Wishy-washy
The Big Toe
The Hungry Giant

Get-Ready Readers
The Party
Go, Go, Go
The Storm
If You Meet a Dragon
Painting
The Tree-house

Jellybean Read-Together Big Books
Cat and Mouse
Wiggly Worm
The King's Pudding
Good Boy, Andrew
Play It Again, Sam

Sunshine Integrated Language Experience
Babby Gets Dressed
Little Brother
I Love My Family
Spider, Spider
Goodbye Lucy
The Cooking Pot

Story Poems
Wave a Wand
If Wishes Were Horses
Jemima

Tales of South Asia
How Things Began
Legendary Creatures
Fools or Wise Men

Starpol Action Series
The Spider
Ghosts of Zol
The Truggs

List 7
(All Readers, Grades K-8)

Jim Trelease's *Read-Aloud Handbook* is a well-known classic in the field of reading. In delightful prose, Trelease describes how to read to children, and then provides an outstanding annotated listing of recommended books for reading aloud. Here are some of Trelease's most highly recommended books.

Picture Books

Alexander and the Terrible, Horrible, No Good, Very Bad Day by Ray Cruz
The Animal by Lorna Balian
Bedtime For Frances by Russell Hoban
Bennett Cerf's Book of Animal Riddles by Bennett Cerf
The Book of Giant Stories by David Harrison
Goodnight Moon by Margaret Wise Brown
Hans Andersen - His Classic Fairy Tales translated by Erik Haugaard
If I Ran the Zoo by Dr. Seuss
Little Bear by Else Holmelund Minarik
The Little Engine That Could by Watty Piper
Make Way for Ducklings by Robert McCloskey
Mother Goose, a Treasury of Best Loved Rhymes Edited by Watty Piper
Norman the Doorman by Don Freeman

Short Novels

Among the Dolls by William Sleator
Dexter by Clyde Robert Bulla
Freckle Juice by Judy Blume
Grandma Didn't Wave Back by Rose Blue
Inside My Feet: The Story of a Giant by Richard Kennedy
Warton and Morton by Russell Erickson
The Wonderful Story of Henry Sugar & Six More by Roald Dahl

Novels

The Black Stallion by Walter Farley
Caddie Woodlawn by Carol Ryrie Brink
Charlotte's Web by E.B. White
Cricket in Times Square by George Selden
The Enormous Egg by Oliver Butterworth
Lassie Come Home by Eric Knight
The Search For Delicious by Natalie Babbitt
The Twenty-One Balloons by William Pene du Bois

Poetry

At the Top of My Voice by Felice Holman
Casey At the Bat by Ernest Thayer
Is Somewhere Always Far Away? by Leland B. Jacobs

Where the Sidewalk Ends by Shel Silverstein

Anthologies

Animals Can Be Almost Human, Compiled by Reader's Digest
The Fairy Tale Treasury, Collected by Virginia Haviland
Science Fiction Tales: Invaders, Creatures and Alien Worlds, Edited by Roger Elwood

List 8
(All Readers, Grades K-12)

These books from Harper & Row are part of a superb collection. The catalogue is wonderful. Each book is described fully, and many of the books are multiple award winners. This partial listing of excellent books for recording is available from: Harper Junior Books Group, 10 East 53rd Street, New York, NY 10022.

Books For Ages 3-8

The Emperor's New Clothes by Hans Christian Anderson
Anno's Counting Book by Mitsumasa Anno
A Three Hat Day by Laura Geringer
Me and Neesie by Eloise Greenfield
Bedtime for Frances by Russell Hoban
Bread and Jam for Frances by Russell Hoban
What Do You Do Dear? by Sesyle Joslin
Amelia Bedelia by Peggy Parish
The Three Sillies and 14 Other Stories to Read Aloud by Anne Rockwell
Let's Be Enemies by Janice May Udry
Science Toys & Tricks by Laurence B. White, Jr.
Red Fox and His Canoe by Arnold Lobel
The Case of the Hungry Stranger by Crosby Bonsall
Mouse Tales by Arnold Lobel
Fossils Tell of Long Ago by Aliki
How to Talk to Your Computer by Seymour Simon

Books for Ages 8-12

Mummies Made in Egypt by Aliki
Where Do I Belong? A Kid's Guide to Stepfamilies by Buff Bradley
Queen of Hearts by Vera Cleaver and Bill Cleaver
Science Experiments You Can Eat by Vicki Cobb
In the Year of the Boar and Jackie Robinson by Bette Bao Lord
Sarah, Plain and Tall by Patricia MacLachlan
It's Like This, Cat by Emily Cheney Neville
Unriddling by Alvin Schwartz
Runaway to Freedom, A Story of the Underground Railway by Barbara Smucker
Little House in the Big Woods by Laura Ingalls Wilder

Books For Ages 12 & Up

Sounder by William H. Armstrong
Don't Worry, You're Normal by Nissa Simon
I Hate School: How to Hang In and When to Drop Out by Claudine G. Wirths and Mary Bowman-Kruhm
Dragon of the Lost Sea by Laurence Yep
The Magical Adventures of Pretty Pearl by Virginia Hamilton

The Contender by Robert Lipsyte
The Upstairs Room by Johanna Reiss

List 9
(All Readers, Grades 5-12)

Arthea J. Reed's recent book, *Comics to Classics*, was a much needed resource for teachers of older students. This excellent book lists and describes favorite books of students in Grades 5-12. It was published by the International Reading Association (Newark, Delaware), in 1988. These are some of the books on Reed's list.

Animals
"The Bear," by William Faulkner in *Three Famous Short Novels*.
The Black Stallion by Walter Farley
The Incredible Journey: A Tale of Three Animals by Sheila Burnford

Black Heroes
The Autobiography of Miss Jane Pitman by Ernest Gaines
If Beale Street Could Talk by James Baldwin

Death
Close Enough to Touch by Richard Peck
When the Phone Rang by Harry Mazer

Fantasy
Animal Farm by George Orwell
The Lion, the Witch and the Wardrobe by C.S. Lewis
A Wrinkle in Time by Madeleine L'Engle

Folklore, Legend, Myth, and Religion
Beauty: A Retelling of the Story of Beauty and the Beast by Robin McKinley
Seven Daughters and Seven Sons by Barbara Cohen and Bahija Lovejoy

Handicaps and Illness
Go Ask Alice, Anonymous
Lisa, Bright and Dark by John Neufield

Humor
Huckleberry Finn by Mark Twain
Half Nelson, Full Nelson by Bruce Stone

Love and Romance
Beginner's Love by Norma Klein
I Stay Near You by M.E. Kerr

Mystery
Tales of a Dead King by Walter Dean Myers

Science Fiction
Deadeye Dick by Kurt Vonnegut
The Martian Chronicles by Ray Bradbury

Short Stories
Early Sorrow: Ten Stories of Youth, Edited by Charlotte Zolotow
Sixteen Short Stories by Outstanding Writers for Young Adults, edited by Donald R. Gallo

References

Barchas, S.E. *I Was Walking Down the Road,* New York, NY: Scholastic, 1975.

Biro, Val. *The Emperor's New Clothes,* San Diego, CA: The Wright Group, 1986.

Candappa, Beulah. *Tales of South Asia: Legendary Creatures,* San Diego, CA: The Wright Group, 1986.

Carbo, Marie. "A Word Imprinting Technique for Children With Severe Memory Disorders," *Exceptional Children,* Vol. 11, Fall 1978a, pp. 1-5.

Carbo, Marie. "Teaching Reading With Talking Books," *The Reading Teacher,* Vol. 32, December 1978b, pp. 267-273.

Carbo, Marie. "Making Books Talk to Children," *The Reading Teacher,* November 1981, Vol. 35, pp. 186-189.

Carbo, Marie. *Reading Style Inventory® Research Supplement,* Roslyn, NY: LRA, 1988, pp.1-4.

Carbo, Marie. "Recorded Books = Remarkable Reading Gains," *Early Years K-8,* Vol. 15, November 1984, pp. 44-47.

Carbo, Marie. "Advanced Book Recording: Turning it Around for Poor Readers," *Early Years K-8,* Vol. 15, January 1985, pp. 46-48.

Carbo, Marie. "Deprogramming Reading Failure," *Phi Delta Kappan,* November 1987, pp. 197-202.

Carbo, Marie, Rita Dunn and Kenneth Dunn. *Teaching Students to Read Through Their Individual Learning Styles,* Englewood Cliffs, NJ: Prentice-Hall, 1986.

Ceprano, M. "A Review of Selected Research on Methods of Teaching Sight Words," *The Reading Teacher,* Vol. 35, December 1981, pp. 314-322.

Chomsky, Carol. "After Decoding, What?" *Language Arts,* Vol. 53, March 1976, pp. 288-296.

Cobb, Lauren. "Hong Kong: Get it While it's Hot," *Suitcase Talk,* published by Lincoln Tour and Travel, Vol. 15, No. 6, Winter 1988/89.

Gag, W. *Millions of Cats,* London, England: Faber and Faber, Ltd., 1929.

Hoban, Russell. *Bread and Jam for Frances,* New York: Harper and Row, 1964.

LaShell, Lois. "Teaching Handicapped Children to Read Through Their Individual Reading Styles," Report presented at Seattle-Pacific University, Seattle, WA, 1983.

Lauritzen, Carol. "Oral Literature and the Teaching of Reading," *The Reading Teacher,* Vol. 33, No. 7, 1980, pp. 787-790.

Little Bear, Little Bear, Portland, Oregon: Nellie Edge Big Books, 1989.

Lobel, Arnold. *Mouse Tales,* New York: Harper & Row, 1972.

Markham, James M. "Gorbachev Says Change Will Sweep Bloc," *New York Times International,* July 6, 1989.

Parish, Peggy. *Amelia Bedelia,* New York: Harper & Row, 1963.

References

Torgesen, Joseph K., William E. Dahlem and Jonathan Greenstein, "Using Verbatim Text Recordings to Enhance Reading Comprehension in Learning Disabled Students," *Learning Disabilities Focus*, Vol. 3, No. 1, 1987, pp. 34-38.

Wirths, Claudine G. and Mary Bowman-Kruhm. *I Hate School: How to Hang In & When to Drop Out*, New York: Thomas Y. Crowell, 1987.

Notes

Notes

Notes

Notes

Notes

Notes